RIDING WITH ROSSER

By
Major General
Thomas L. Rosser

Divisional Cavalry Commander,
C.S.A.

Edited by S. Roger Keller

 Burd Street Press

This Burd Street Press publication
was printed by
Beidel Printing House, Inc.
63 West Burd Street
Shippensburg, PA 17257-0152 USA

In respect for the scholarship contained herein, the acid-free paper used in this book meets the guidelines for permanence and durability of the Committee on Production Guidelines for Book Longevity of the Council on Library Resources.

For a complete list of available publications
please write
Burd Street Press
Division of White Mane Publishing Company, Inc.
P.O. Box 152
Shippensburg, PA 17257-0152 USA

Library of Congress Cataloging-in-Publication Data

Rosser, Thomas Lafayette, 1836-1910.
    Riding with Rosser / by Thomas L. Rosser : edited by S. Roger Keller.
        p.   cm.
    Includes bibliographical references and index.
    ISBN 1-57249-066-7 (alk. paper)
    1. Rosser, Thomas Lafayette, 1836-1910. 2. United States-
-History--Civil War, 1861-1865--Personal narratives, Confederate.
3. United States--History--Civil War, 1861-1865--Campaigns.
4. Generals--Confederate States of America--Biography.
5. Confederate States of America. Army--Biography. I. Keller, S.
Roger, 1931- . II. Title.
E470.R67 1998
973.7'3'092--dc21
[B]   97-37107
                                                                CIP

PRINTED IN THE UNITED STATES OF AMERICA

TABLE OF CONTENTS ————————————————————

Thomas Lafayette Rosser

I am indebted to Mr. and Mrs. Douglas Cochran, of Hagerstown, Maryland, for the major contents of this book. While its size is small, its contents are enormous. It contains General Thomas L. Rosser's personal account of the Civil War. The material is believed to have been clipped from a Charlottesville, Virginia, newspaper by family members and carefully guarded over the years by the Cochrans. The articles are reprinted exactly as they appeared at that time, and are not edited except to fill in names etc. Footnotes attempt to augment some events not made especially clear or that are not included.

In them, we are permitted a rare glimpse into the general's thoughts on the war, and the men who fought alongside him to the painful end. Rosser was tall, and muscular, with broad shoulders. His eyes were dark brown, and his hair and moustache were black. A superb horseman, he was always elegantly mounted.

Rosser was a native of Campbell County, Virginia, born on a farm, October 15, 1836, the son of John and Martha M. Johnson Rosser. The family moved to Texas in 1849, where he received an appointment to West Point Military Academy in 1856, where the course of study at that time was for five years. Rosser was in his graduating year, and within only two weeks of receiving his diploma, when he was ordered into the field by President Abraham Lincoln. He resigned and went directly to Montgomery, Alabama, where he was commissioned a first lieutenant in the regular army of the Confederate States.

His service began as an instructor to the Washington Artillery of New Orleans. Later, he commanded the second company of that organization at the Battles of Blackburn's Ford and Manassas, in 1861. Later, with Maj. Gen. J. E. B. Stuart in the Battles of Munson's

Hill and Lewinsville he performed with brilliant capability. Rosser won a promotion to captain when he skillfully shot down one of General George McClellan's observation balloons in the Peninsula Campaign. At the Battle of Yorktown he commanded his battery in the defense of that area and all along the route of retreat up the peninsula. At the Battle of Mechanicsville he was severely wounded and upon his return to active duty, was soon promoted to lieutenant colonel of artillery. A few weeks later Rosser was given command of the Fifth Regiment of Virginia Cavalry, by Stuart. Thereafter he followed a brilliant 15-month career as a dashing and brave cavalry officer, which he writes about here. During this period he served with distinction and proved himself a skillful and intrepid officer, with consummate skills.

He commanded the advance of Stuart's expedition at Catlett's Station, in the campaign against Brig. Gen. John Pope, in which he captured the general's horse and orderly. At Groveton, Virginia, August 28, 1862, his was the only cavalry with General "Stonewall" Jackson. Here, he confronted and held in check the forces of Brig. Gen. Fitz John Porter, on August 29. At South Mountain, in Washington County, Maryland, his was the only cavalry at Crampton's Gap, and along with Pelham's artillery played a prominent part in the fighting. He participated in the Battle of Sharpsburg or Antietam, and later commanded Fitz Lee's Brigade of cavalry in the fighting against General Pleasonton's Federal cavalry.

Along with Stuart and Pelham, Rosser was on court-martial duty at the opening of the Battle of Kelly's Ford, Virginia. Returning immediately to their troops they determined the Confederate situation greatly deteriorated. Rosser located his regiment to the rear of the lines, and ordered a charge upon the Federals who were beginning to drive the front lines back. His bold charge stopped the enemy advance and sent them reeling backwards. In the ensuing fight Rosser was wounded again and Pelham was killed.

He remained disabled until the Pennsylvania campaign of 1863. After the Battle of Gettysburg he was promoted to brigadier general and given command of the "Laurel Brigade," the old command of Turner Ashby. Rosser led this rugged and distinguished command brilliantly into the Confederacy's twilight days of 1864.

At Trevilian Station he drove his great friend from his days at West Point, George Armstrong Custer, back on Fitz Lee and his Virginians, and captured a large number of prisoners, but was painfully wounded in a charge.

Rosser was prematurely declared the "Saviour of the Shenandoah Valley" in 1864. The title held little meaning after another bloody clash with Custer, this time at Tom's Brook, Virginia, on Sunday, October 9, that culminated in his defeat. Despite the loss he was promoted to major general on November 1.

Rosser earned highest praise from his superiors for his efforts against Sheridan's superior forces in the valley, and in commanding Fitz Lee's division at Cedar Creek, where he saved Early's army. He held the line and checked the enemy's pursuit until late in the day when he took a position in the works at Fisher's Hill and safely conducted Early's retreat to New Market.

Rosser used his imagination in battle, at times pulling off brilliant and confounding movements in the face of extreme adversity. When Col. William C. Wickham was wounded at Warrenton, Rosser was given command of his brigade in the absence of Fitz Lee. Rosser suddenly found Federals in his front and in his rear as well, and using much cleverness, he sidestepped them, returning his men to safety without one empty saddle.

His raids into West Virginia were acknowledged textbook examples of dogged determination and outstanding leadership, as, for instance, with 300 men he captured two infantry regiments at Beverly. His campaigns there, at New Creek and Moorefield, only served to enhance his already brilliant reputation.

In 1865 he maintained his standard of excellence commanding a division of cavalry, fighting with honor in Virginia at Five Forks, and at the High Bridge, on the retreat toward Appomattox and Lee's surrender. On April 6, he captured the entire command of General Read, who fell in combat. Then, after daylight on the ninth, Rosser captured General David Gregg and rescued a wagon train near Farmville.

When the end came at Appomattox, Virginia, he was with General Robert E. Lee, but did not surrender. He skillfully eluded the Federals, including his friend Custer, west of Appomattox Court House, and broke through the Federal lines with two regiments of his cavalry. The war ended for him and his men on May 2, with their capture.

Prior to the 1863 Christmas holiday, Rosser married Miss Bessie Winston, of Hanover, a daughter of Mr. William Winston and a first cousin of Revolutionary War patriot, Patrick Henry. Present at this joyous occasion were John Pelham, Jack Garrett, Jim Deering, John Fountaine, Pierce Young, Fitz Lee and Jeb Stuart, most notable for his bright yellow sash, and flowing plume. And, of course, there were numerous renditions of Stuart's favorite song, "If you want to have a good time, jine the cavalreeee." And lots of laughter too as the cavaliers joined in on the rollicking, "Old Joe Hooker, come out of the Wilderness."

Mrs. Rosser lived with her husband in winter quarters in 1863–64, at Culpeper and Orange Court House, and frequently rode with him, sometimes up to 40 miles a day, along picket lines.

His financial condition after the war was in a shambles, and it was with the same dogged determination he exhibited on the field of battle, that he regained his position of honor and respect in his community.

He went first to Baltimore where he had military friends and was employed by the city government as an engineer. In that capacity he made a survey and plat of the harbor. Later he was employed by the Baltimore and Ohio Railroad Company as a sub-engineer in the construction of its McConnellsville Branch.

He served for a time as superintendent of the National Express Company under General Johnston, and was later named chief engineer for two railroads: the Northern Pacific and Canadian Pacific. Each benefited from his outstanding work ethic as they opened the west to rail travel and transport. Here he was reunited again with his old friend Custer, whose troops would occasionally guard his surveying parties.

When the Spanish-American War began, President William McKinley commissioned him a brigadier general and gave him command of the Third Brigade of U.S. Volunteers, in the Second Army Corps under Brig. Gen. James H. Wilson. The appointment was confirmed in June 1898.

Rosser died at "Rugby," his Charlottesville, Virginia, home, near the University of Virginia, March 29, 1910, at 7:45 p.m. It was four years after he had suffer a stroke, leaving him unable to speak. Those present at his death included Mrs. Rosser, her three children, including Mrs. C. C. Cochran, their families, and other relatives. Services were held in the Charlottesville Presbyterian Church with burial in Riverview Cemetery.

In the following pages you will read Gen. Rosser's account of the war, in which he was wounded nine times! Here, in his words, is the American Civil War as viewed by one the Confederacy's most competent and brilliant officers. You will journey with him to the plains of Manassas, into the Wilderness, to Sangster's Station, up and down the Shenandoah Valley battling Gen. Phil Sheridan, contesting his friend at West Point, George Custer, struggling at Spotsylvania Court House and Trevilian Station. Thrill to his capture of 2,500 head of Federal cattle, his surprising victory at New Creek and the sad, frantic account of the war's final days.

Saddle up! Here is a breathtaking journey into America's fascinating past, with a man who was there and in the very middle of its magnificent panorama of action.

Now, it's time to "Ride with Rosser!"

S. Roger Keller
Hagerstown, Md.
March 1996

CHAPTER 1

ANNALS OF THE WAR
Chapters of Unwritten History
Rosser and His Men
Of Saddles Emptied and Sabres Lost in the Last
Years of the War
On the Plains of Manassas
Battles in the Valley
by Major General Thomas L. Rosser
Division Cavalry Commander Under Early

Soon after the close of the war of secession I was requested by General Wade Hampton to prepare and furnish to him a narrative on my operations while serving as brigadier and major general in the Cavalry Corps of the Confederate States Army of Northern Virginia. I was also requested by General Fitz Lee to prepare such a narrative for him. But, having found myself, at the close of the war, penniless, with a young family on my hands to support and children to educate, I really did not have the leisure to rake over the past and to collect the facts required of such a purpose. Yet the duty which I felt that I owed to the brave men of my command who had so bravely fought the battles and who had so patiently suffered and endured the hardships of fatigue and hunger in the defense of their homes, their honor, and their native land, prompted me, when the request was made, to make an effort to comply with it and I sent the result to General Hampton in 1866, but it was very hastily prepared and, upon the whole, so unsatisfactory to me that for a long time I have been seeking an opportunity for writing another, and as

1

the first has never been published I hope the General will allow this to go in its stead.[1]

Early Service and Promotion

In the beginning of the war I was commissioned first lieutenant in the Confederate States Artillery, but was soon elected captain of the second company of the celebrated battalion of the Washington Artillery, of New Orleans, commanded by that accomplished soldier, Colonel James R. Walton.

I served with this command through the campaign of 1861 around Washington and upon the Peninsula and rose to the rank of lieutenant colonel of artillery. Being wounded on the retreat from Yorktown, [May 1862] I did not return to the army until the beginning of the Seven Days' battles around Richmond [June 25, 1862]. Then I was promoted to colonel of the Fifth Virginia Cavalry, and I was serving in this capacity when, on 15 October 1863, I was appointed brigadier general. This was by birthday, the day on which I was 27 years old—older it is true, than Napoleon was when he took command of the army of Italy, yet when I was assigned to the command of the renowned Laurel Brigade, I must confess that I wished that I was an older man.

The Laurel Brigade

This brigade was composed of the Seventh, Eleventh and Twelfth Regiments and Col. E. V. White's Battalion of Virginia Cavalry. This brigade had been organized and trained to fight by the immortal Turner Ashby.[2] The rank and file composing this brigade, with a few exceptions, were young men. They were well armed and well mounted and won upon many a hard-fought field and exalted reputation for gallantry and efficiency and they were justly proud of their excellent name. When General Ashby was killed [June 6, 1862] General Beverly Robertson was given command of the brigade. When he was transferred to the South, General W. E. Jones had the good fortune to command it, but his valuable services being required in southwestern Virginia, this brigade was given to me.[3]

ON THE MANASSAS PLAINS

The Affair at McLean's Ford, with Mention of General Pryor's Gallantry

Our army was in pursuit of General [George Gordon] Meade [commanding the Army of the Potomac] and I assumed the command of the Laurel Brigade on the Plains of Manassas. Colonel E. R. Funsten, of the Eleventh [Virginia Cavalry Regiment], had been in command since we left the Rappahannock and the brigade had done excellent service under his able direction since the pursuit of the Federals began. It was reported to us that the Federal commander had greatly reduced his force by allowing the men to go home "to vote the Republican ticket," and when General R. E. Lee threatened his flank the enemy retired upon the fortifications covering the vicinity of Washington. The cavalry pursued as far as Bull Run and upon arriving there the enemy was found in position on the high ground beyond the stream.

Seizure of McLean's Ford

I had been marching in the rear of the corps and knew but little of what was occurring in front. That portion of the corps that was in my front halted a mile or so south of McLean's Ford and formed in an old field, which was grown up in scrub pines. I got up to the front about 4 P.M. and was at once informed by a staff officer of General J. E. B. Stuart [commanding the Confederate cavalry corps] that I was required to take possession of McLean's Ford which was at that time in possession of a small force of the enemy's infantry. I ordered the command to dismount and while this was being done rode to the front, where I could see the nature of the ground along the creek and the position of the enemy at the ford. Returning to the command I deployed it as skirmishers, and moving at a double quick took possession of the line of the creek each side of the ford, but suffered heavily in doing so from the fire of the infantry and artillery on the hills beyond. As soon as I got possession I notified General Stuart of the fact and anxiously watched for the coming of the command in my rear, which I supposed intended to cross, but to my infinite disgust, after remaining for an hour under heavy fire and sustaining heavy loss, I was notified by General Stuart that I had better fall back. When this word reached me most of my men had gotten in the stream for protection and were firing over the banks on the enemy, and although in a very uncomfortable position they were well protected.

A "Charge to the Rear"

There was a constant danger, however, of the enemy, who was a vastly superior force, rushing upon us and capturing or destroying us in the stream. As night was near at hand, and desiring to extricate myself before darkness set in, I determined to adopt the suggestion of Stuart and fall back, but it was not an easy matter to do, for I knew that the enemy would charge upon me upon the receipt of the slightest intimation of my purpose of retiring. A signal for retreat was agreed upon and a trusty man was sent along the line in the water to notify the company commanders. The signal was the charge, but instead of doing so were to "charge to the rear!" The enemy, however, was on the alert and discovered the ruse as soon as my men rose from the creek and pursued us rapidly. My horses had been brought up from under cover of the pines to within a few hundred feet of the creek, and being so hotly pursued by the enemy, there was danger of a stampede of the horses before we could mount them.

In crossing the creek the enemy's line was more or less broken and I took advantage of this circumstance to check the advance. I called a halt and an about-face, but found great difficulty in stopping my men and turning upon the enemy, but in this task I was greatly assisted by General Roger A. Pryor, who but a short time before, had resigned his position as brigadier general on account of some disagreement with the President [Jefferson Davis] and had taken his position among his neighbors and friends as a private soldier in one of the companies. Forgetting that he was only a private soldier Pryor seized a flag, planted it upon the ground and called on the men to stand by it. His example was instantly followed by a large percent of the men and I was thus able to check the enemy and hold him there until support could be brought up to assist me in withdrawing and mounting.

General Meade halted his army in the vicinity of Bull Run, and General R. E. Lee returned to his old position on the Rapidan and the Rappahannock. As we were slowly falling back, covering the rear of General Lee's army, we were overtaken on the 19th of October by the Federal Cavalry under General Judson Kilpatrick. I was attached to Hampton's division which was under the immediate command of General J. E. B. Stuart, Hampton being absent on account of wounds received at Gettysburg. Stuart was retiring along the Warrenton and Alexandria Turnpike. Fitz Lee was moving back with his division parallel to and near the Orange and Alexandria Railroad. There was no one following Fitz Lee, and, as Kilpatrick pressed up the turnpike in pursuit of Stuart, Lee saw a good opportunity for striking him a good blow on his flank and rear. Lee's plans were communicated to Stuart and they were concurred in. Lee was to cross over the pike and when Stuart heard his guns he was to turn around and attack as vigorously as possible.

Like the Irishman's Flea

Late in the afternoon we heard the guns of Lee immediately in the rear of Kilpatrick and when we turned upon him every man felt that we should completely destroy "Kill's" whole command; but the wily "Kill" was not thus to be caught.[4] We went thundering down the pike midst clouds of dust and Fitz Lee came up the pike under like circumstances. We met, but Kilpatrick had fled without roads or without order through the woods and across Broad Run without fords and had escaped, leaving only a few prisoners and half a dozen portable forges in our possession. We spent some time in trying to find where Kilpatrick had gone. Finally we found his trail and chased him until dark without bringing him in or without inflicting much punishment on him. Had we remembered the tactics which "Kill" used at Brandy Station a few days previous to this, when attacked in front by Stuart, from Culpeper Court House, and [Col. Lunsford L.] Lomax [Eleventh Virginia Cavalry] and Fitz Lee, from Stevensburg, we should have been better prepared to fund him after he suddenly left the road. "Kill" had learned how to "scatter" to avoid pursuit in his "raid on Richmond,"[5] in May, and whenever he got into a close place this was the tactic he employed. We might have pursued him rapidly with a portion of our force and inflicted great punishment upon him. After dark several squads of lost men came to us, mistaking us for their friends. They had become bewildered in their scattered flight and were unable to follow their general.

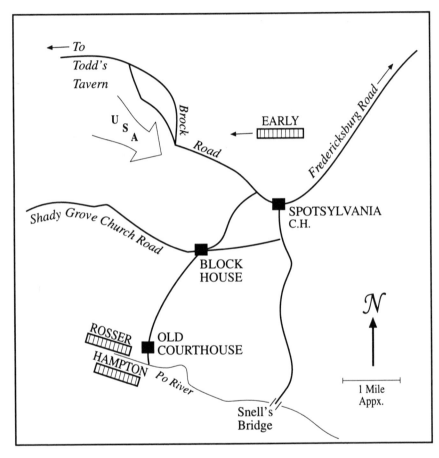

Spotsylvania, May 8, 1864

Map by S. Roger Keller

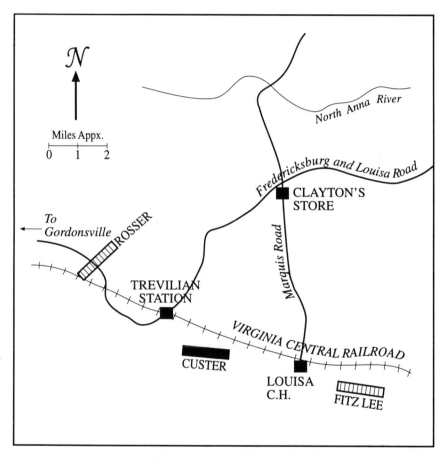

Trevilian Station, June 11, 1864

Map by S. Roger Keller

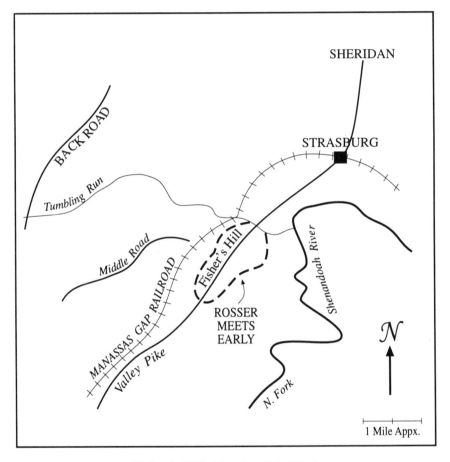

Fisher's Hill, October 19, 1864

Map by S. Roger Keller

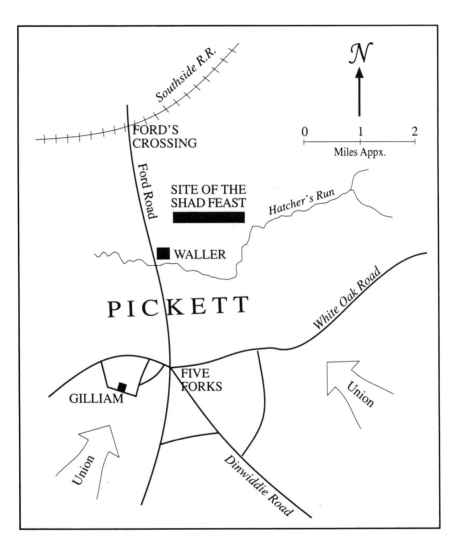

Five Forks, April 1, 1865

Map by S. Roger Keller

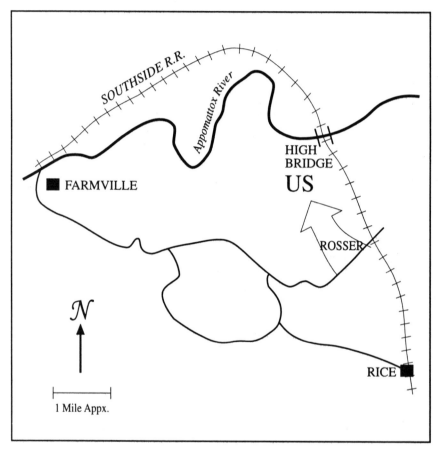

Fight Near the High Bridge, April 6, 1864

Map by S. Roger Keller

CHAPTER 2

IN THE WILDERNESS
Winter Experiences Among the
Tangled Forests of Spotsylvania County

After this we were not further disturbed by the enemy and we resumed our old position on the Rapidan and the Rappahannock. My command was then sent to Fredericksburg and I was charged with picketing the fords from Germanna to Fredericksburg and to watch the river as far east as Port Royal. About the middle of November the enemy returned to his old position near Culpeper Court House and sent his cavalry out to cover his front along the Rapidan. On the 17th of November I was ordered by General Hampton to move my brigade to Charlottesville, and when I arrived there, late in the afternoon, I was met by General Hampton, who had only his staff with him, and informed me that he desired to go with me across the Rapidan to see where the enemy was. After nightfall we crossed the river at Germanna Ford and marched in the direction of Stevensburg and just about daylight we surprised a camp of a regiment of cavalry near that place. We captured the camp, sixty prisoners, one hundred horses and several wagons. My loss was one man killed and two wounded. This expedition was simply a reconnaissance to ascertain the position of the enemy and we were not strong enough to meet the entire cavalry force of the enemy, which our night dash through the pickets had put in the saddle. Therefore as soon as we had gathered up the captured property and loaded it into the captured wagons, we returned unpursued to our side of the river.

11

On the Orange Plank Road

On the morning of the 26th of November the enemy moved across the Rapidan in force, crossing at Ely's and Germanna Fords, and took position in the Wilderness along Mine Run. The roads through this region are few, narrow and rough. The soil is so thin and unproductive that the region is uninhabitable, and it is grown up with an underbrush which is almost impenetrable, hence it is properly called "The Wilderness." A plank road had been constructed from Fredericksburg to Orange Court House before the war, but this was now old, decayed, and worn and almost impassable. As soon as my pickets reported that the enemy was crossing the river in force I conveyed the intelligence to the commanding general (R. E. Lee) and moved my command to Todd's Tavern, from which post I could best observe the enemy's movements and at the same time cooperate with any movement of our army against him. During the night my scouts reported that the enemy was moving on the plank road towards Orange Court House, and that he had neglected to take the precaution of leaving a picket on the Brock Road leading to Todd's Tavern, where I was lying. Therefore on the morning of the 27th I moved out on the Plank Road, where I found and captured a portion of the ordnance train of the Fifth Army Corps.

Stampede in the Forest

Upon my appearance there was a general stampede among the mules and the teamsters, every teamster whipping his mules into a run, the lightest loads and fastest mules passing those more heavy and slow, but all exerting themselves to the utmost in an effort to get in front and escape. Many teamsters seeing that escape was impossible, abandoned their teams and saved themselves by running into the woods; but the road was soon blocked for miles and many wagons were upset and broken. Some of the mules were entangled in harness and down and unable to get up. Many others had freed themselves from the wagons and were running and wildly braying through the woods. I secured and sent to the rear all the wagons that I could extricate from the blockade and was burning the remainder when a Federal brigade of infantry was hurried to the spot at a double-quick and, deploying in the dense woods, drove me off. I withdrew as I had gone in, via Todd's Tavern, with my herd of loose mules and a large number of wagons and continued my march to Jack's Shop, near Verdiersville.[1]

An Estimate of Meade

On the 28th the entire cavalry command under General J. E. B. Stuart moved around the enemy's left, and with my brigade in front, attacked the enemy at Parker's Store, where we captured a few prisoners and discovered that the enemy was extending his left flank. We therefore returned during the night and covered the roads leading toward Gordonsville. The next day we were in the saddle at daylight and hung upon the enemy's left flank, all day, expecting him to attack. General R. E. Lee held his entire army on the qui vive all day, expecting battle, but to our disgust, we found on the morning of the 30th, that the enemy had hastily retreated during the night and a most excellent opportunity for defeating him had been lost.[2] General Meade was a good engineer, a brave and efficient lieutenant, but was not a captain, and as commander of the Army of the Potomac he was "another failure." The Battle of Gettysburg was without plan so far as Meade was concerned. The Federal Army at Gettysburg was very strong numerically, composed of veterans and well organized under good corps and division commanders, and posted on the heights it served as a wall against which General Lee unwisely exhausted his strength, crippled his army and had to retreat, while if he had practiced, as he was competent to do, any skilled maneuver against Meade, he would have forced him from his position, and if he had not overtaken and beaten him before reaching Washington the great battle of the war would have been fought in sight of the capital of the nation, and with what result God alone knows.

HURRYING TO THE VALLEY
A Winter March, During Which the Enemy
Is Stuck at Sangster's Station

After the farce in the Wilderness our troops resumed their old position. I took my brigade back to Fredericksburg. On the 16th of December [1863] I was informed by General R. E. Lee that there was a small force (a regiment or two) of the enemy moving [south] up the Shenandoah Valley from Winchester towards Staunton. This small force was to be a diversion of the enemy in aid of [Brig. Gen. William Wood] Averill [Federal cavalry commander] who was then making a raid upon the Virginia and Tennessee Railroad. I was directed to cross the Shenandoah River in the rear of his command and prevent its escape. I received this information and order about noon and as the Rappahannock River at Fredericksburg could only be forded at low tide, I assembled my command on its banks before dark and waited for the tide to go out. This occurred about dark and although the water was very deep, we forded, only the smallest horses swimming. I took no carriages with me, but a few ambulances, and carried five days' rations in haversacks. On the morning of the 17th it began to rain very hard and fearing that the streams in my front would be flooded and impede my march, I pressed on as rapidly as it was safe to urge the horses. Upon reaching the Occoquan I found it rising rapidly and already quite full, but I found a shallow ford at Wolf Run Shoals. It was night when I got across the Occoquan. It was still raining hard and had been doing so continuously all day.

At Sangster's Station

In my anxiety to cross the railroad without delay and to hurry on to the Shenandoah before it should be unfordable, I procured a guide who could take me straight through the country where there were no roads, and consequently no guards to molest me or to occupy my time; but the night was so intensely dark and all the streams so very high that I abandoned this plan and pushed on to Sangster's Station, where I knew the enemy had a small force guarding the railroad bridges at the station. As I approached the railroad station I came to the bank of a small stream which was running rapidly and evidently very deep and on the opposite side stood the stockade of the enemy almost immediately in my path. The Seventh Virginia was in front. The enemy had discovered us before we reached the stream and a challenge and a shot from the sentinel on duty at the stockade warned me that I had no time to examine the ford, but should act promptly.

Capture of the Stockade

I ordered Colonel Richard H. Dulaney to take his regiment [Seventh Virginia Cavalry] across the stream and attack the stockade, but at the command only the gallant Captain [Daniel C.] Hatcher and his splendid [First] squadron [Seventh Virginia Regiment] succeeded in making the crossing, the remainder of the regiment by some means missed the ford and passed down the stream without crossing. The next regiment, the Eleventh, was close at hand and seeing the mistake of Dulaney, I ordered Lt. Col. [Charles H.] Ball, who was commanding the Eleventh, to take his regiment to Hatcher's assistance and, although the enemy by this time was thoroughly aroused and was pouring sheet after sheet of fire into the head of Ball's column, the gallant old regiment went surging through the water and in a moment was up the hill on the other side and the stockade was ours.

Gallantry of Ball and Hatcher

In crossing the creek the gallant Captain [M. B.] Cartmell [Company B, Eleventh Virginia] was killed and a number of his men and horses were wounded. The intelligence, valor, and promptness displayed by Col. Ball and Capt. Hatcher on this occasion saved me a great deal of trouble and placed these two other officers very high upon the roll of merit in my estimation, and I rejoice to say that from that dismal night to the close of the war Ball and Hatcher and their gallant followers never faltered or failed when called upon on the battlefield to carry their sabres into the ranks of the enemy.

After the capture of the stockade some time was consumed in carrying for the killed and the wounded and collecting the prisoners. After these important matters had been attended to I continued the march and the drenching rain continued to fall.[3]

Among the captures on this occasion at Sangster's Station was a very beautiful flag presented by the city of New York to the One Hundred and Sixth-fourth Regiment of New York Volunteer [Infantry], and a silver bugle. The bugle I gave to the gallant Hatcher's squadron and through Colonel Ball and his gallant regiment I presented the flag to the Virginia Military Institute, and recently (1883) the same flag has been returned to the mayor of New York by the corps of cadets of the Virginia Military Institute, and by him returned to its old regiment.

Continuation of the March

Marching all night I halted at Upperville about daylight to have breakfast and to feed the horses, which occupied about an hour's time. Then I resumed the march for Berry's Ferry, but when I reached the river I found it very high, and its great width and rapid current defied even the thought of an effort to swim my command across it. The rains had ceased but all roads but the macadamized pikes were muddy and rough. I knew that my affair at Sangster's had aroused the enemy at Culpeper and I expected him to close upon my heels in pursuit, and here I halted on the banks of an impassable river with my brigade hungry, drenched and weary.

My mind was now bent, not on how best to cross the Shenandoah and capture the party mentioned in General Lee's order, but how best I could escape with my own command from the enemy now in pursuit of me. I had been in the saddle now two days and one night. I had marched rapidly and the men and horses required food and rest.

WITH GENERAL EARLY
Cavalry Operations in the Valley in
December 1863, and January 1864

The enemy might possibly pursue me towards Berry's Ferry, but the heavy rains might enable him to foresee the impossibility of my crossing the Shenandoah and the necessity of my marching up the river. Therefore, I feared that I would be intercepted at Front Royal or Luray, and this danger necessitated a continuance of my already forced marching up the right bank of the river. I continued to do this and reached Luray a few hours before a division of the enemy's cavalry passed through Thornton's Gap just behind me, and I was safe. The river was still very high, but I succeeded in fording at Conrad's Store and joined General Jubal A. Early at Mount Jackson on the twentieth, having marched 230 miles in seventy-two hours. On reaching General Early I learned that the party which I had been sent against had returned to Winchester and that General Fitz Lee had returned from an unsuccessful pursuit of General Averill, and it was ordered that Fitz Lee should take the cavalry into West Virginia to collect beef cattle for rations for General R. E. Lee's army.

All of us required a few days' rest, and the horses needed shoes. The patriotic citizens in the neighborhood supplied us with forage and rations and on the morning of the 27th of December we crossed North Mountain on our way to Moorfield in search of beef. The weather was very cold and there was a great deal of ice on the mountains and our progress was very slow. The people in Moorfield and the adjacent valley were enterprising and prosperous and were, during the war, devoutly attached to the Southern cause, and they were always ready to welcome the coming of the Confederate Corps and divided freely and liberally with them all that they possessed. Consequently, there was no coercion necessary in collecting beeves from these good people. After making our mission known to the citizens themselves, we proceeded to the valley of Patterson's Creek where we captured a small wagon train of thirty-five wagons,[4] which were en route under a small escort to Petersburg, on the south branch of the Potomac above Moorfield, where there was a small garrison. After capturing this train of wagons and sending them back to the valley under a sufficient escort, we proceeded down Patterson's Creek about thirty miles and collected a few hundred head of beef cattle and some sheep. Then we returned to the valley, Fitz Lee rejoining the Army of Northern Virginia, and I remained with General Early, who had been placed in command of the Valley District.

On the Potomac

Having recuperated somewhat from the fatigues of the previous month, on 27 January 1864, General Early ordered me to take my brigade, Gilmore's Battalion, and McNeill's Rangers over North Mountain to Moorfield, and he followed with Thomas's Brigade of infantry. I reached Moorfield on the morning of the 29th and began the construction of a bridge over the Potomac for the infantry to cross, but while thus engaged a scouting party of the enemy from Petersburg discovered us, and fearing that our presence might be reported to the enemy at New Creek, I sent a detachment over to

Patterson's Creek to intercept any party on the road between the two posts. Early on the morning of the 30th I moved my command over the mountain, with the view of investing the fortified position of Petersburg.[5]

A Brush on the Mountain

When I reached the top of the mountain I saw a small party of the enemy who were obstructing the road by which I was marching by felling trees across it and cutting away the retaining walls where they were supporting the ground on steep hillsides and otherwise endeavoring to render the road impassable, but I intercepted them too soon. They had just begun their work and I dismounted the Twelfth Regiment [under Maj. Thomas E. Massey] and drove them off, but not without a spirited skirmish, in which Major John Heck of my staff was painfully wounded by a musket shot through the thigh. After the Twelfth had driven off the obstructing party the road was speedily repaired and my command passed through to the valley where we found a train of ninety-three well-loaded wagons under an escort of about a thousand infantry awaiting my arrival. I mounted the Twelfth under Maj. Massey and put it to the rear of the enemy, and with the artillery and the remainder of the brigade dismounted I attacked the train's escort in front.

Capture of the Train

After a few shots had been fired by the artillery I advanced my line rapidly upon the enemy and when within easy range they broke and ran to the mountains, many of them throwing away their arms. I captured the entire train as it stood in park, and it was a rich prize, too. Every wagon was new, well loaded with rations and drawn by fat mules. Some of the teamsters ran off with the command to the mountains, in which case I detailed soldiers to take their traces and then sent the train over the mountain under a guard to General Early, who was still at Moorfield. I then moved up the valley and encamped near Petersburg, as it was too late to attack the place that night. Early the next morning I marched into Petersburg and found that the enemy had evacuated the place during the night and escaped by a blind road that I knew nothing of, and made their way to New Creek. General Early marched up from Moorfield and joined me on the morning of the 31st [of January, 1864] at Petersburg.

After Cattle

From Petersburg I returned down Patterson's Creek and followed it to its confluence with the Potomac and collected all the beef cattle found on the way. Fearing the enemy might get in my rear from Romney, I left Col. Thomas Marshall in command of the Seventh at Mechanicsburg Gap and with the remainder of the command I pushed on to the Potomac. At the mouth of Patterson's Creek I found a guard of fifty men, whom I captured, and then I destroyed the railroad bridge over Patterson's Creek and did all the damage I could to the iron bridge across the Potomac and then returned safely to Moorfield with my prisoners and 1,200 head of fat beeves for the hungry soldiers under General Lee on the Rapidan.[6]

At Mechanicsburg Gap

While I was at Patterson's Creek, General Averill attacked Colonel Marshall at Mechanicsburg Gap and the gallant colonel was also attacked by a force of cavalry from New Creek. After a hard fight he had to abandon the gap and retire towards Moorfield without being able to communicate this fact to me. For some unaccountable reason the enemy did not attempt to cut me off and I escaped without firing a shot. Before reaching the spot where I had left Marshall I sent scouts ahead, to see if all was right, and they returned to report the enemy was in my front, and my situation appeared most critical. I halted and closed up the command. I put beef cattle under the command of Major [E. H.] McDonald of the Eleventh, than whom a better or braver soldier never pressed a rein, and then compactly, and the advance squadron with sabres drawn, I boldly moved ahead.

Looking for Averill

It was a very dark night and I calculated to dash into Averill with all of my strength. If I failed to clear the road I would at least so paralyze him that I could get around him and escape with my men, if I had to abandon my beeves. I had left the artillery with General Early and had nothing on wheels, but when I reached the position where I expected to find Averill across my path, he was gone. I was the happiest man that ever rode on that road. After Marshall had withdrawn from the gap, General Early had become very uneasy about me, but was too far off to render me any assistance. When I returned to him safely, with my captures, he too was a happy man.[7]

Averill followed us the next morning but did not get close enough to become engaged in any fighting. We then returned to the valley and I was sent with my brigade to Rockbridge County to spend the remainder of the winter, for the purpose of recuperating my command. At Falling Spring, in the midst of abundant supplies of forage and rations and among wealthy, cultivated, and patriotic people, I remained until the last of April. During this short time (two and one-half months) a great many of my sick and wounded men returned to me. My horses got fat and my effective strength increased from twelve hundred to twenty-three hundred men.[8]

On the 1st day of May 1864, General Stuart informed me that the enemy under General Grant had crossed the Rapidan and directed me to move down the valley and cross the Blue Ridge Mountain at Stanardsville Gap, thence move to Orange Court House where other instructions would be received. I complied with this order with as much alacrity as circumstances would admit of, and reached Orange Court House about noon of the 4th, where I found an order from General Stuart for me to move down the Plank Road toward the Wilderness until I reached our army in position, then to put myself in communication with him. I continued the march in obedience until I reached Verdiersville, which was late at night. There I found General Stuart, who directed me to rest there that night, and move early the next morning on the Catharpen Road and join Fitz Lee, who was supposed to be at Todd's Tavern.

My supply train had been delayed by the usual blockade of wagons which filled the roads in the rear of the army expecting battle and did not reach me that night, but I had anticipated a contingency of this kind and every trooper had been required to carry in addition to his own ration, one day's ration of corn in a sack tied behind his saddle for his horse. In our service the men owned their own horses and, of course, were careful with them. My men were all good citizens, and consequently they were good soldiers and made a guard house in my command a useless thing. I don't remember even having a case of disobedience to deal with, and all orders given for the purpose of increasing the efficiency of the command were obeyed with the utmost alacrity. There was no murmuring or grumbling heard from the men, and while this is more than I can say of some officers, upon the whole, I think there was never in any service a finer, more cheerful and more efficient brigade than the "Old Laurel Brigade." General Grant, who had made a name for "bull-dog tenacity" in his campaign against Vicksburg, was commanding the enemy in our front and we hitched our horses to the young trees along the roadside and threw ourselves on the ground to rest till morning, feeling sure that the morrow would usher in a day of bloody strife.[9]

A Clash with Wilson

At daylight on the 5th [May 1864] I was in the saddle and moved out as directed by General Stuart to join General Fitz Lee at Todd's Tavern. I moved with as much caution as I should have done if I had not been informed that Fitz Lee's Division was in my front, and I was wise in proceeding thus cautiously, for I had been marching for only a short time when I met the enemy face to face in a narrow road. I was riding with the advance squadron, commanded by Captain Louis Harman, when we came upon him. Harman had just been promoted from the position of adjutant of the regiment to that of captain of one of the excellent companies of the Twelfth [Co. I], and he was a young, but intelligent and dashing officer. At the first sight of the enemy I ordered the charge and before the enemy could make any preparation for defense, Harman was upon them with the sabre.

Rout of the Northerners

The road was narrow and the country on each side of it was covered with very dense underbrush and a small growth of oaks, and I saw at a glance that numbers would avail nothing and that only heads of columns could meet and, consequently, the best material would prevail; therefore, my confidence in my own troops assured me victory. I followed the first blow with the second and third as rapidly as I could bring up the squadrons in succession and thus gave the enemy no time to recover himself or to deploy for defense, and soon he was fleeing before me in the wildest disorder and rout. From the prisoners I learned that it was Wilson's Division of Cavalry that I was chasing. [Lt. Col. James Harrison Wilson]

There was an occasional clearing or little fields of a few acres by the roadside, in which I would find small detachments drawn up for resistance, but when I came upon them they broke and fled without offering much hindrance to my rapid pursuit. Just before reaching Shady Grove Church, Wilson employed the tactics which Kilpatrick availed himself of at Buckland by abandoning the road, scattering and escaping through the woods on the "every man for himself" plan. I crossed the Po River at the old windmill and followed the train of the "flying artillery" several miles in the direction of the old Wilderness Church, but as the day was far spent, and I knew I must be near the main body of Grant's army, I gave up the chase of those scattered troops, collected my own men, and returned to the Catharpen Road about a mile east of Shady Grove Church.

Custer Struck the Same Way

As I came into the road I met Custer's Brigade going to the relief of Wilson. [Brig. Gen. George Armstrong Custer, commanding the 2nd Brigade of Brig Gen. Judson Kilpatrick's 3rd Cavalry Division] I applied the same tactics to Custer that I had so successfully used against Wilson a short time before—charged him on sight—but found that this did not work so well on Custer. My first blow staggered him, but he soon recovered himself and repulsed me. My men and horses being jaded by the long, running fight which we had just had with Wilson, we really were not in condition to meet fresh troops, but I had posted my reserve well when I charged Custer, and when he repulsed my charge I was ready with another regiment and met his charge with the charge. We closed in a hand-to-hand fight, in which each command scattered to the right and left in the woods, where each dismounted and bushwhacked away at each other until after dark. Custer retired to Todd's Tavern and I withdrew to Shady Grove Church, where I bivouacked for the night and had my supply wagons brought up with forage and rations.

The Day's Work

My loss in this day's work was one hundred and forty-six men killed and wounded. I also sustained a great loss in the capture by the enemy of the gallant Captain Harman, who lost control of his spirited horse in the first charge and was carried headlong into the lines of the enemy. [Harman was held prisoner until near the end of the war.] I captured many prisoners and horses, but do not remember the number, and killed a great many of the enemy's horses and killed and wounded a great many of his men. In looking back on this day's events I feel that I was most fortunate. I reached the theater of war late in the evening before, much fatigued by my long march from the valley. I knew nothing of the position of the enemy and was sent by the chief cavalry officer of the army to a definite place, where I was told by him that I would find my friends. I was not so much cautioned to look out for the enemy, and meeting him and beating him under such circumstances was certainly quite as much as could have been expected of me.[10]

With Stuart

About daylight on the morning of the 6th General Stuart came galloping into my bivouack calling for Rosser. "Where is Rosser?" I rose from the fence corner where I had slept a short distance from the road and called to him to know what was the matter. He appeared to be in a great hurry and ordered me to get my men in the saddle at once and go to the front with him; he was unattended except by his staff. Before sunrise I was in motion, but instead of moving to the right to connect with Fitz Lee I was conducted off to the left of Todd's Tavern and required to make an effort to connect with the right of General R. E. Lee's line of battle. General Stuart rode at the head of the column with me and we were preceded by only a few troopers who rode ahead of us on the narrow, blind road through the thick brush as an advance guard. We had marched in this way about three miles from Shady Grove Church, when our party in front reported to me that the enemy was forming a line of cavalry in a small field just in front of us. The brush was so thick that General Stuart and I, after halting the brigade, rode to the front and watched the enemy unobserved from the edge of the brush and not a thousand feet from him. The enemy's force was superior in numbers to mine, but it was decided that I should attack him, and I moved the brigade to the front, where we were sitting, and ordered Colonel E. V. White to make a dash into them with his intrepid little battalion [35th Virginia Cavalry].

Col. White's Charge

Col. White was but a boy in appearance, but he was as brave as the trusty sabre in his hand. In the campaigns with the immortal Stonewall Jackson in the valley he had been literally shot to pieces, and his brave manly heart endeared him to his men. He was a superb horseman and was always well mounted, possessed of a most graceful figure, and with long wavy hair he nearly approached the ideal knight of ancient chivalry than any man I ever saw on the field of battle. When ordered to charge, Noland-like, all he ever wanted to know was "Where is the enemy?" and on this occasion when I pointed to the enemy, twice his strength, and ordered him to make a dash at them, right into them he went with his little battalion, utterly regardless of their ability to take his life or hurt his men. Such intrepidity never fails.

Effect of the Charge

The force of White's blow laid many of the enemy prostrate and hurried the remainder back into the thick underbrush whence they had come. White's horse, being shot, fell on him, and while he was being extricated the enemy turned upon his battalion, but the remainder of the brigade checked their advance and they then dismounted in the woods and checked our further advance upon them. My command was then dismounted and deployed as skirmishers and the artillery was brought into battery. The remainder of the day was spent in wasting ammunition, firing into the woods at an unseen foe, and I must say that to my mind the day was very unprofitably spent, so far as our troops were concerned.[11]

General Stuart

General Stuart was killed at Yellow Tavern a few days after this, while gallantly opposing a force [under Lieut. Gen. Philip H. Sheridan] greatly superior to his own, and no cavalry soldier of the Confederate States army should attempt to throw the faintest shadow upon the brightest escutcheon of so patriotic and gallant a man as General J. E. B. Stuart; yet all of us who participated in the Gettysburg campaign know that the mistake committed by him then in leaving General R. E. Lee without "eyes" and "ears" and riding aimlessly about the country, not knowing where our army was, and without striking the communication of the enemy, contributed largely to our failure at Gettysburg. All of us know that the cavalry under Stuart in the Wilderness was more of a tax than an assistance to the army under General Lee, for it had to be fed and was too much scattered to participate in the battles and was not able to concentrate upon Sheridan when he attacked our communications with Richmond. If our cavalry had been held in reserve at some point in rear of our army and the flanks watched by small detachments, Sheridan might have been buried in the Chickahominy. I also think that if the cavalry had been with General Lee as he approached Gettysburg the battle would not have begun at Cashtown and the Battle of Gettysburg would not have occurred at all, but the armies would have met on ground selected by General Lee, and the result would therefore have been more favorable to our side.

SOUTHWARD WITH LEE
Events from the Spotsylvania Battle
Till After the Fight at Haw's

During the night of the 6th my scouts reported no cavalry in my front, and as General Stuart had left me I reported the fact to General R. E. Lee. Early the next morning I joined my line with General Longstreet's on my left and holding my reserve upon the Catharpen Road I threw out flankers, videttes, and scouts to observe and report any movements of the enemy. During the night of the 7th General Lee extended his right as far as Spotsylvania Court House to confront the left wing of Grant's army, which had been moved in that direction. On the morning of the 8th one corps of the enemy moved up the Catharpen Road from Todd's Tavern in the direction of Shady Grove Church. To meet and oppose this advance I took a line of defense along the Po River where General Hampton joined me with the other two brigades (Butler and Young) of his division. The enemy showed no disposition to force our position, and nothing more than a skirmish at long range between sharp-shooters and some artillery practice was engaged in. As this corps of the enemy lay in our front, his flank was exposed to an attack from General J. A. Early, who was still in position in the Wilderness, and this fact being reported to General Lee, Early was directed to attack him. About 4 o'clock in the afternoon, at an agreed signal, Early attacked him in flank, while Hampton attacked with his division in front and the enemy was driven back towards Todd's Tavern with considerable loss.[1]

The Battle at Spotsylvania

Grant then drew in his right and held the line of the Ny River, confronting General Lee at Spotsylvania Court House, and in this position the most terrible fighting was carried on between those opposing armies, day and night, that the history of the human race gives any account of. In this memorable battle my command contributed its full strength, fighting principally dismounted, as the woods were too dense for cavalry to operate in mounted form. The heaviest of this fighting occurred on the 12th of May, beginning a little before daylight. This was the occasion of Hancock's dash over our breastworks and his capture of General George H. Stewart and "Allegheny" Johnson, and it was here in the front of General Rhodes, where forest trees, a foot in diameter, were shot down by bullets. One of these, an oak, can now be seen in the Ordnance Museum at Washington D.C.[2]

Operating on Grant's Right

On the 15th I was ordered by General Hampton to make a forced reconnaissance in Aldrich's direction on the Plank Road, for the purpose of ascertaining the position of Grant's right. In executing the order, I encountered a brigade of cavalry at Piney Branch Church, which after a spirited resistance, retired in the direction of Aldrich and took position behind the old railroad embankment, in which position I deemed it unwise to attack him, but I turned to the right and penetrated as far as the poor house, near which I found the right of General Grant's line of infantry.

On the Little River Ny

On the 9th [May 1864] General Ewell was ordered by General Lee to attack the enemy near the poor house. The cavalry division, under General Hampton, accompanied by him, but the country was so grown up with underbrush and the roads so narrow and the crossing of the Ny River so bad for transporting artillery that General Ewell did not go into position to attack till late in the afternoon. By then our movement had been discovered and we were not able to surprise the enemy, but found him ready to receive us. Our attack produced no important results, and as soon as it was dark we returned to the south side of the Ny. The enemy continued to extend his left toward Richmond after he had failed to drive General Lee out of his way, and inch by inch he crept, crab-like and sidewise, toward our right.

Near Wright's Tavern

On the morning of the 21st [May 1864] General Hampton moved his division of cavalry in the direction of Milford, but kept on the south side of the Mattapony River, the other divisions of the cavalry corps having gone off in pursuit of Sheridan. On reaching Wright's Tavern, my brigade being in front, I found a small force of the enemy's cavalry which had retired across the Mattapony River. After firing a few shots at my approach in the direction of Milford, and in pursuing this force I ran into a large force of infantry and artillery, which convinced us that the whole of Grant's army was in motion toward Hanover Junction. Hampton posted his division in front of the enemy, so as to impede his progress as much as possible, and to give General Lee time to transfer his army from Spotsylvania to Hanover.

At Haw's Shop

On the 22nd the enemy moved upon Hampton in force and compelled us to retire beyond the North Anna River, where General Lee was then forming his line of defense. The cavalry was then moved to the left of our position and we guarded the fords and scouted the country so as to discover any changes which the enemy might make in his position. Grant did not attempt to cross the South Anna, but moved down the Pamunkey River and crossed at Nelson's Ferry and Hanovertown. As soon as Grant started crossing to the south side of the Pamunkey, Hampton moved the cavalry corps to Enon Church, and on the 28th to Haw's Shop, attacked the cavalry under Sheridan, who had rejoined Grant after his raids on the railroads.

Disposition of the Brigades

The country at Haw's Shop is not unlike that about Spotsylvania, mostly of the chapparel order and not favorable to the maneuvering of cavalry. General M. C. Butler, of South Carolina [2nd Cavalry Regiment, Hampton's Brigade] had lost a leg in the Battle of Brandy Station and had not sufficiently recovered to resume command of his brigade, and the senior officer Colonel Rutledge, commanding the brigade, was directed to report to me. I commanded the center, Fitz Lee the right and W. H. F. Lee the left. The enemy was in position, dismounted and Grant's whole army was in close supporting distance in his rear. I dismounted the Laurel Brigade under the command of the senior Colonel R. H. Dulaney, and held Colonel Rutledge in reserve. As soon as I moved my line into the woods I encountered the enemy's strong force with carbines and artillery, and I was unable to dislodge him, even after I had brought up my reserve under Rutledge. The enemy, seeing that we were either unwilling or unable to advance, endeavored to drive us and made a most determined effort on that portion of my front commanded by the gallant Colonel Thomas Marshall of the Seventh

Virginia. Our right and left wings were also held in check by the heavy lines of the enemy.[3]

Col. Marshall's Gallantry

The fire of artillery and carbines in front of Marshall was unusually heavy, and fearing that he would not be able to hold out against it I sent a staff officer to him to know how long he could hold out, and the splendid old soldier replied, "Until my last man falls," and there he stood upon the most exposed position of his line with a pleasant smile upon his face, giving his orders as cheerfully as if the tragedy in which he was acting was only a practical farce. Hampton's objective in attacking the enemy so vigorously at Haw's Shop was doubtless to ascertain his position and strength, and the enemy, fearing that our attack was backed by a movement of General Lee's entire army, threw his entire cavalry and a corps of his infantry and artillery into the fight for the purpose of developing the nature of our attack, or the whole thing may have been the result of an accident. We found the enemy strong and fought him hard, certainly.

The Value of Such Fighting

The question has often been discussed as to whether it is proper or productive for cavalry to indulge in such fighting as this on its own hook. It is true that no battle should ever be fought without a plan and a purpose; still it sometimes happened that an effort to reestablish a disturbed picket post brought on a general engagement between the opposing cavalry corps of the two armies. The country in eastern Virginia over which Grant and Lee operated was not favorable to cavalry, and finding but little use for his strong corps of this area around Richmond and Petersburg, Grant sent his cavalry to the valley, where the country was more open and more suitable for its service. General Lee was compelled to send his there to oppose him, and in my opinion, General Hampton should have been sent with them and the entire command of the valley troops should have been given to a cavalry general, because the cavalry arm in the operations there played the most conspicuous part.[4]

THE FIGHT AT ASHLAND
A Brush in Which Private Conrad Fairly Earned
The New Rank of Major

After the affair at Haw's Shop the enemy came forward and occupied the line of the Totopotomoy Creek and his cavalry guarded his flanks, but the main body of it lay on the right flank next to Hanover Court House. General Hampton collected our cavalry near Atlee's Station on the Virginia Central Railroad, and picketed the roads off toward the enemy's position and kept scouts hovering near his lines to report all his movements. Receiving information on the first of June that the enemy was at Hanover Court House, I was sent on a reconnaissance in that direction with my brigade, but without artillery. When I reached the road leading from Peak's Station to Ashland I discovered that the enemy's cavalry, at least a brigade strong, had but a few moments before gone to Ashland. I reported the fact at once to General Hampton and started in pursuit. I soon overtook the enemy and at the first dash captured several prisoners, from whom, greatly to our delight, we learned that we were again after McIntosh's Brigade, a portion of the command of our old Catharpen friend, General Wilson.

At the Heels of McIntosh

My men were very enthusiastic and as soon as we came up with the main body of the enemy we charged him, capturing over two hundred prisoners, with their prisoners and arms, and drove the enemy before us. In my rapid pursuit of the enemy my small force soon became greatly thinned out and scattered, and I was in great danger of being turned upon by the enemy and beaten. I halted my brigade to allow those on slow horses in the rear to close up, but before this was accomplished I discovered that the enemy had reformed about a regiment and was moving back upon us; only a portion of the Eleventh Regiment was near me at the time and with this I moved to the front to meet the enemy as he approached me. When we got to within a hundred yards of each other the Federals halted and my men did the same. Each seemed to dread a collision. The Federal officers rode in front of their men and vainly called on their men to follow, and my efforts and those of my officers to urge my men on were also fruitless.

How Conrad Saved the Day

I rode out towards the enemy and begged my men to charge, but all this was of no avail. When I scanned the situation it was quit evident in my mind that whichever side made the attack would win. When all hope seemed to leave me and the enemy had actually begun to advance, a singular circumstance relieved me. Private Holmes Conrad, of the Eleventh Virginia [Co. D], seized the regimental flag and with the sagacity of genius and the courage of Horatio, he rode into the head of the enemy's column, calling to his comrades to follow him and the flag they had so long honored.

Conrad's Unsurpassed Heroism

His example fired the hearts of my men, and instantly every heel was driven into the horses' flanks and my little command moved as one man, and with impetuous madness dashed into the enemy's already wavering column, which broke and scattered in every direction. This act by Conrad was the most handsome exhibition of personal gallantry I ever saw, and as he saved my command and the fruits of victory I showed my appreciation by reporting the fact to the President of the Confederate States the next day and asked that Private Conrad be given a commission. When Mr. [Jefferson] Davis sent me his commission as major in the Confederate States army, stating that it was given as a reward for extraordinary valor and skill on the battlefield, I felt far more gratified than Major Conrad could have felt. I cannot see why Conrad was not killed when he rode in among the enemy; his flag was seized by several men, who endeavored to wrench it from his hand, and when he was rescued and his flag saved, I counted five non-commissioned officers who were killed around the flag.[5]

Death of Young Turner

The enemy retreated through Ashland where it was struck by General Hampton with his other brigades of his division and that of W. H. F. Lee, who drove him at a run towards Hanover Court House, until darkness put an end to the affair. My loss in this engagement was twenty killed and wounded. Among the killed was a very fine young fellow, Thomas Turner, [Co. A, 7th Virginia Cavalry] of Fauquier County, Virginia, who was serving as a courier for me at the time. He was a handsome, gallant, and noble young man, and his death greatly distressed me. It is said that death seeks the "shining star," and all of us who remember his harvests in Virginia too well realize this fact. He was taken as was "the gallant" Pelham, immortalized at Fredericksburg, and the handsome and chivalrous Dearing who was to fall before the end; and after each battle, whether he had won a victory or suffered defeat, we bemoaned the loss of our best men—not only lost to ourselves, but to our army, to our country, and to the world.

An undated postwar picture of General Thomas Rosser
Courtesy of Mr. and Mrs. Douglas Cochran,
Hagerstown, Md.

Rosser married Bessie Winston of Hanover, Virginia, prior to Christmas, 1863. Present for the gala occasion were Jeb Stuart, Fitz Lee, John Pelham, and other famous Confederate military personnel.

Courtesy of Mr. and Mrs. Douglas Cochran, Hagerstown, Md.

Rugby Hall, the Rosser home in Charlottesville, Virginia

Courtesy of Mr. and Mrs. Douglas Cochran, Hagerstown, Md.

Undated postwar picture of General Rosser
Courtesy of Mr. and Mrs. Douglas Cochran,
Hagerstown, Md.

General Rosser during the Civil War
Courtesy of Mrs. Thomas Cochran,
Hagerstown, Md.

An undated picture of General Thomas Rosser
Courtesy of Mr. and Mrs. Douglas Cochran,
Hagerstown, Md.

Sally Rosser, daughter, and one of three children born to General and Mrs. Thomas Rosser.

Courtesy of Mr. and Mrs. Douglas Cochran,
Hagerstown, Md.

CHAPTER 4

BATTLE OF TREVILIAN STATION
The Most Important Cavalry Fight of the War
A Shot in the Leg

After this affair at Ashland we were allowed to remain in bivouac near Atlee's Station until the morning of the 9th, when, learning that Sheridan was moving in the direction of Gordonsville, General Hampton assembled the cavalry corps in light marching order and we started in the same direction. Sheridan had under his command a very large force of cavalry, and the country in which Grant was operating was so very unfavorable to its use that it could well be spared for raids for a distant coup de main [a sudden military movement] when necessary, and when we learned that Sheridan was moving, divined his destination to be Lynchburg and his purpose to be the destruction of the railroad and canal. We moved upon the interior and shorter lines, and our excellent scouts hung upon the flanks of the enemy and kept us accurately informed of his position and movement.[1]

A Faithful Valet

The night before Sheridan marched, after he had given all the orders necessary for putting the troops in motion, a Negro boy of nineteen or twenty years, who was employed as a servant by one of the officers, left camp and came into our lines. Early in the war when I was captain of artillery, he had attended me in the capacity of a valet, and soon as he reached the cavalry pickets he asked to be assigned to me. He reached me late at night, and in a clear and straight forward manner related all that had occurred in Sheridan's

36

camp preparatory for this expedition, and this information was of great service to us. This Negro boy was a slave and when I left the Washington Artillery he was returned to New Orleans by his master. When the city was captured by the Federals he was employed by an officer as a servant and as soon as an opportunity offered itself he returned to the Confederate army in which his master was serving.

The Negroes of the South, as a general thing, have not behaved very well since the war, but it has not been half their fault. The carpetbaggers and political adventurers who flocked to the South during the period of reconstruction, so called, are responsible for all the trouble the Negro man has brought on himself and the Southern people since the war.

The conduct of the Negro slave in the South during the war was commendable in the extreme. All the white men were in the field and their wives, mothers, sisters, and daughters were left at home at the mercy of the Negro slave. At the end of the war between the North and the South the destiny of his race hung, and while armies were struggling upon distant fields of battle he peacefully toiled in the fields and never once raised his hands against the defenseless ones at home.

In Position at Trevilian

On the night of the 10th we encamped two miles west of Trevilian Station and learned that Sheridan was camped on the North Anna, about five miles east of us. Fitz Lee was at Louisa Court House with his division, and Hampton had only the three brigades of his division with him near Trevilian. On the morning of the 11th Hampton marched back to the railroad station, and as it was quite certain that the enemy intended passing along the railroad at that point, [Col. Calbraith] Butler's and [Col. Pierce M.] Young's brigades were out into position to meet him as he came up. I was sent around to the left to oppose any movement against Gordonsville or to act as circumstances might require. I took position at the crossroads about two miles from Trevilian, in the direction of Gordonsville, and sent out scouts to watch the enemy and learn which road he had resumed his march, and while I was waiting I heard Butler and Young engage the enemy.

With Compliments to Custer

My scouts reported no movement toward Gordonsville and I impatiently awaited instructions from General Hampton, who remained at Trevilian. Butler and Young had dismounted their men and sent the horses to the rear for safety. Custer, passing between Louisa Court House and Trevilian, got in the rear unobserved and captured horses, ambulances and wagons, and one of the men escaping came galloping up the road to where I was, without his hat and with a sabre cut across his face, reported these facts to me. I moved back at once at a trot, and coming from a direction where danger was not expected, I surprised Custer, scattered his command and recaptured not only our own men and property but killed, wounded, and captured many of his men and horses. After these disturbances in their rear, Butler and Young were withdrawn to the high ridge west of the railroad, and Sheridan, advancing, took up a defensive line along the railroad track, and for an hour or two there was only light firing along the skirmish line of dismounted men.

Out of the Fight

Late in the afternoon General Hampton made an effort to dislodge the enemy from his strong position, and while leading my brigade against the enemy, who had posted himself behind the railroad embankment, I was badly wounded by having my leg broken just below the knee by a carbine shot, and I was thus prevented from participating further in this engagement. My wound was tied up on the field by Dr. Burton, my "fighting surgeon," who was always at the front, and then I was taken a short distance to the rear, where I remained within hearing distance of the fight until Sheridan was reported retreating, then I was taken over to the James River and Kanawha Canal and thence to Richmond.

Hampton and Fitz Lee

Up to the time I was wounded there appeared to have been very little co-operation between General Fitz Lee and General Hampton, and while I am not prepared to say whose fault it was I felt then, and all of us who were in the fight on the 11th felt, that it was very unfortunate that General Lee did not unite with us that day. He did join General Hampton the next morning, and united, they successfully repulsed Sheridan and caused him to abandon his plans and return to General Grant. The Battle of Trevilian was the most important cavalry fight that occurred during the war. The entire cavalry force of the opposing armies in Virginia met there, many miles away from the support of other troops; each commander was thrown entirely on his own resources. Had Sheridan won the battle he would have gone on to Lynchburg, or wherever he desired to go there would have been no one to oppose him. He could have destroyed railroads, canals, depots, and, indeed, cut General Lee off and starved him out of Petersburg and Richmond.[2]

Sheridan Fairly Beaten

After the death of General Stuart no chief of the cavalry was appointed. When the divisions were together General Hampton, who was the senior officer, took command. I very much question whether

General R. E. Lee put the entire cavalry force of his army under
General Hampton when he sent it in pursuit of General Sheridan. If
he did, I am surprised that Hampton did not bring Fitz Lee to him
on the first day's fight at Trevilian. After the two divisions were
united on the second day (12th), Hampton handled them with consummate skill and Sheridan was fairly and completely beaten, and
all of his apologies for his retreat, "ammunition exhausted and presence of infantry," are unworthy of a great soldier. Why was he there
without ammunition? Didn't he expect to have some fighting? If he
had found a large force of infantry in his path he should have destroyed the railroad, each side of it, and thus compelled it to march
back, while he could have ridden off unmolested upon the duties
for which he was sent. These excuses are really too ridiculous to be
discussed.

REAM'S STATION AND RED TAVERN
Fighting and Riding South of the James in the
Last Week of Summer

My brigade was commanded in my absence by Colonel R. H.
Dulaney, and I hope the record of his gallant services at Salem,
Sappony, and Jack's Shop will some day be published. Recovering
sufficiently to allow me to get about on crutches, I returned to the
field on the 22nd of August and resumed command of my brigade,
which was then encamped near Monk's Neck bridge, in front of
Ream's Station, south of Petersburg. On the 23rd the enemy drove
in the cavalry pickets of Hampton's Division, then under the command of Brigadier M. C. Butler, who was the senior officer of the
division, and the entire division was ordered to cross Rowanty Creek
at Monk's Neck bridge and support the picket reserve which had
been driven in.

Upon crossing the creek I found Butler's Brigade in line, and
halting my command I rode to the front to find General Butler. The
enemy was not advancing, but seemed disposed to hold the ground
we had but recently occupied and the railroad line. Butler informed
me, when I found him, that he proposed to attack with every man
he had and, if possible, ascertain the strength and purpose of the
disturbing party. This seemed to me a wise decision and I prepared
my command for action at once, and the attack was most vigorously made and the enemy was driven nearly back to Ream's Station, uncovering a large force of infantry.

The Fight at Ream's Station

The presence of this force was presented to General Lee at
once, and Lt. Gen. A. P. Hill was sent from Petersburg with his
corps to drive it back. General Hill crossed the Rowanty at Monk's
Neck bridge the next day and late in the afternoon attacked the

enemy at Ream's Station. The cavalry under General Hampton crossed at Malone's bridge and attacked on Hill's right. The enemy was driven with little difficulty, and but for the lateness of the hour of our attack we would have done the enemy very great damage. Our cavalry, fighting on foot, drove the enemy's infantry and made a great many captures. Just about dark we found a large number, several hundred, of the enemy in a field having thrown away their guns, who were all huddled together and appeared to be lost. The night was very dark and the cavalry had to give up the chase in the woods. After Hill had broken up the enemy so badly and if the cavalry had been used mounted, the enemy would have suffered far more than he did. It is true that the country is not favorable to the employment of cavalry, yet I believe that all fleeing troops should be given the sabre. What Sheridan did with his cavalry at Cedar Creek, Hill might have done at Ream's Station with his; but I fancy that none of us knew in season that there was an opportunity for such a use of cavalry or the full extent of damage we had done the enemy, for I confess that I was surprised at their demoralized condition when we overtook them with dismounted cavalry about dark.[3]

Red Tavern

On the 1st of September I made a reconnaissance in the rear of Grant's army near the Red Tavern, drove off the enemy and captured their camps and drove the infantry outpost guards inside their entrenchments. I found the army as grand and as well fortified from the rear as from the front; the troops were not only covered by a good breastwork but strong abatis [barricade of felled trees with sharpened branches] was planted along the whole line and all the roads used in communicating with and supplying the troops were constructed between these two strongly fortified lines. Sheridan and his cavalry had been sent to the valley to look after General Early, who was threatening Washington from that direction, and one division under General Gregg was all the cavalry that General Grant had with him, while General Lee had two divisions, Hampton's and W. H. F. Lee's (Butler and Young's Brigades had been sent south to cooperate with General Joseph E. Johnston).[4]

CAPTURE OF CATTLE
A Herd of Nearly 2,500 Fat Steers Taken without Asking from the Federals

Our army was and had been for some time on short rations, and as our cavalry was stronger than that of the enemy, we were determined to forage in the rear of the enemy's position. Scouts reported a large herd of cattle near Coggins' Post, and on the morning of the 14th of September, General Hampton took Dearing's Brigade and mine and General W. H. F. Lee's Division and by making a long detour, crossing the Jerusalem Plank Road at Belcher's Mill, and marching the 14th and day and night of the 15th, we halted near daylight on the 16th as we were nearing the enemy's lines, to dispose of our troops for the attack upon the enemy and the capture of the beeves. W. H. F. Lee was sent to the left towards Prince Georges Court House to amuse Gregg and keep him off. Dearing was sent to threaten Cabin Point and I was ordered to break through the line at Sycamore Church and secure the cattle.

At Sycamore Church

These preliminaries already arranged, I resumed the march. The moon had set and although the sky was cloudless, the night in the woods was very dark. My men were ordered to march in silence, but the road was hard and in the profound stillness of the night the tramp of the horses could be heard a long distance. I knew it would be impossible to surprise the enemy and therefore made my arrangements to fight. I knew that I would find a regiment of cavalry at Sycamore Church and I knew that every man would be in position and ready for me on my arrival there. I brought up the Twelfth Virginia Regiment and gave orders to the commander Major [John L.] Knott, a very gallant officer, to charge just as soon as he was challenged by the enemy.

A Warm Greeting

My guide reported to me that we were near the church, and I was riding by the side of Knott, telling him how to proceed in the event of his being able to dislodge the enemy, when, as if by the flash of lightning, the front was all ablaze by the flash of musketry. The gallant Twelfth was not the least bit staggered by the sudden discharge in its face, as quick as though the charge had sounded the noble, old regiment went thundering on the enemy. But, a strong abatis had been thrown across the road, over which cavalry could not pass, and when it was reached the men dismounted and were put to work clearing it away. Seeing this I dismounted the next regiment, the Seventh, and ran it up in line as skirmishers, and soon cleared the way for the mounted men. The Twelfth was followed by the Eleventh and Twenty-fifth Battalion, and before the enemy could mount and escape, or communicate with the guard over the cattle, they were our prisoners.

The Prize in Sight

When we captured the regiment at Sycamore Church it was barely light enough to see the road, and leaving a strong guard with the prisoners I pressed on in search of the cattle. I had proceeded about a mile when, through the dim light of the early morning, I saw a line of cavalry, about two squadrons, drawn up on a hill in front of me. My command was not closed up and I had to halt for a few minutes, but with a portion of White's Battalion coming up we made a dash at this little squad, which broke on our approach, and pursuing, we soon came upon the beeves.

A Stampede

When I came in sight of the beeves they were running rapidly in the direction of the James River. The herders had thrown down the fence of the corral, and by firing pistols and yelling, Indian fashion, had stampeded the cattle that were running like mad. I ordered the Seventh Virginia, which had just overtaken me, to run their horses until they got in front of the herd then to turn upon it and stop. This order was not easily obeyed, for the young steers ran like buffalo, and it was requiring too much of a jaded cavalry to force it into a race like this. After running a mile or so the steers slackened off their pace and the cavalry was thus able to get in front of them, and then to "round them up," then quiet them, turn them about, and start them to the pens of their new masters on the Dixie side of the line. When the excitement was all over and the herd was obediently following "the leader," I had them counted and found that our prize had amounted to twenty-four hundred and eighty-six head, and all were fat, young steers.[5]

The Return

Notwithstanding the precautions taken by General Hampton of sending General W. H. F. Lee in the direction of General Gregg's cavalry, I was afraid that a portion at least of the Federal Cavalry would be sent down the Jerusalem Plank Road to intercept our herd of beeves and give us some trouble. I, therefore, sent Col. E. V. White and his battalion at a trot to Belcher's Mill, with instructions to hold the position until I reached him with the balance of the brigade. White moved with his usual promptness and reached the point indicated just as the enemy got there, but White was able to secure the desired position, which by nature was a strong one, and by dismounting his men he was able to hold it against a force much larger than his own. There was a large mill pond on his left and a swamp on his right, and the Plank Road was the only avenue by which the enemy could attack White. After the gallant Colonel got into position he sent a messenger to me saying that the enemy was in force in front of him, but his position was a good one and he could hold it.

A Brisk Action

Notwithstanding my confidence in White, I carried on, and when I reached him late in the afternoon I found him warmly engaged with the enemy, who had also dismounted, and was pushing through the swamp on his right, and would soon have outflanked him and compelled him to withdraw. I put the other regiments in position to meet this flank movement of the enemy, and my whole command was soon fighting dismounted cavalry and artillery, but I succeeded in holding the enemy. About sunset General Hampton and the remainder of the command came up, bringing artillery, and thus reinforced we drove the enemy back across the swamp, and after dark we resumed our march.

Pleasantries

The enemy heard during this fight that we had captured the cattle and the remarks that were exchanged between the lines were very amusing. The Federals would call out, "Say, Johnny, when you want a square meal come over and we will give you one," and from our side: "Well, Yanks, when you get another lot of fat cattle let us know and we will come over for them."

"How is living on sassafras tea and fighting for your rights in the Territories, Johnny?"

"How do you like fighting for the nigger and paying tax on tobacco and whiskey?" our boys would reply.

After this affair we saw nothing more of the enemy on this expedition and we quietly resumed our camps along the Rowanty and delivered to General Lee's commissary every one of the 2,486 beeves.

ATTACKING SHERIDAN
Orders from General Early and How They Were
Obeyed as Well as Possible

On the 28th of September I was ordered to move my brigade to the valley of Virginia and report for duty to Lieutenant General J. A. Early, who had just suffered a series of reverses and was then confronting a superior force under General Sheridan, near Harrisonburg.[6] I marched at once, and when I reached Lynchburg I received a telegram from General Early directing me to join him with my staff by rail as soon as possible, and have my brigade march under the command of the senior colonel. I, therefore, turned the command over to Colonel R. H. Dulaney and instructed him how to march.

I took Captain John W. Emmert and Lieutenant P. B. Winston of my staff, with our horses, and got on the cars at Lynchburg, and proceeding by Charlottesville to Waynesboro, I joined General Early at Mount Sydney the 2nd of October. Upon reaching General Early I was placed in command of Major General Fitz Lee's division of cavalry, General Lee being absent, having been disabled from wounds a short while before in the Battle of Winchester. The weather had been wet, and the unpaved roads were very bad. The valley pike, although badly worn by hard usage and having received no repairs during the war, was still a good and broad road, but the other roads, farm roads and back roads, blind roads and no roads at all, such as the cavalry and its transportation were compelled to use, were wretched. When I took command of Fitz Lee's cavalry division, I was ordered to report directly to General Early and not to General Lomax, who was my superior ranking cavalry officer, and who was commanding General Early's other cavalry division. I found the Federals under the command of our old Trevilian friend, General Sheridan, and his three cavalry divisions, commanded respectively by Powell, [Brig. Gen. Wesley] Merritt and Custer, all under the command of General [A. T. A.] Torbert.

In Pursuit of Sheridan

Sheridan was encamped near Harrisonburg and his cavalry confronted mine along the North River. My brigade, under Dulaney, reached me near Bridgewater late on the night of the 5th of October [1864]. Early on the following morning I crossed the river in pursuit of Sheridan, who had broken camp during the night and was then retreating down the valley to avoid a battle with General Early, who had been reenforced by General [Joseph B.] Kershaw's Division of infantry and my brigade of cavalry. This hasty retreat of Sheridan down the valley led General Early to believe that he was leaving the valley and taking his command to Petersburg to reenforce Grant, who had thus far been unable to dislodge General R. E. Lee from his position in front of Richmond and Petersburg. General Early therefore ordered me to pursue with my division as rapidly as possible and to get "beyond Sheridan and to impede his march in every manner I could and discover what his intentions were." I was directed to move upon the "back road" and General Early moved his infantry and artillery on the pike. It may be well to state that there are three roads running all the way through the Shenandoah Valley and parallel to each other—the pike, the middle, and the back road. The middle and back roads are both rough, but the back road, being near the foot of North Mountain, is especially so and the movement of artillery and other carriages over it is necessarily slow. My command, pursuing Sheridan, was composed of my brigade, [Brig. Gen. William C.] Wickham's and [Brig. Gen. W. H. F.] Payne's brigades, the latter two composing Fitz Lee's division, that had been through the fights at Winchester and Fisher's Hill where they had been much worsted, and were consequently greatly weakened by the loss of horses killed and wounded. My own brigade was small. It had been marching and fighting almost continuously since April, and the long march from Petersburg to the valley, only the day before completed, had nearly exhausted my poorly fed horse. My division, all told, did not exceed three thousand men in the saddle.

At Close Quarters

I overtook the rear of Custer's retiring column late in the afternoon of the 6th, near Brock's Gap, when a spirited skirmish ensued, in which I captured a few prisoners. Custer halted, took position, and posted his artillery on the high ground on the opposite bank of Dry River, and thus stood me off until darkness of night gave him an opportunity for withdrawing and continuing his retreat. During the night my scouts came in and reported Sheridan's entire army was near me, and I knew I would overtake it early the next morning and that I could not ride over it or around it with my small force. Not knowing General Early's plans I wrote him that I had overtaken Sheridan, and had seen and engaged at least one division of his cavalry. Realizing that my little division could accomplish but little against such large odds, I requested that he give me written instructions, and on the morning of the 7th I received the following from General Early:

Harrisonburg, Va., September 6th, 1864

General Rosser, commanding cavalry on Back Road:

Press on and get into the rear (front) of the enemy and destroy his trains, for he is running out of the valley. Yours truly,

J. A. Early
Lieutenant General

I fully appreciated the perils of my situation, but determined to obey General Early's order at the hazard of losing my command, for he allowed me no direction in the matter.

THE TORCH OF DEVASTATION
Troopers with Homes in the Valley, Angered at the Sight of Blazing Houses

I moved on the morning of the 7th [September, 1864] at daylight, and following the enemy as rapidly as I could, overtook him about 3 P.M. near Mill Creek. The barns, mills, stacks of wheat, oats, shocks of corn and in many instances the dwelling houses, wherein were sheltered only defenseless women and little children, had all been set on fire by the order of the commander of the Federal troops. The smoke from these fires hung over us like a dense fog, and so concealed my command as it came up that I fell upon the enemy's rear before he knew that I was near. Under cover of the smoke I sent Dulaney with my brigade around on the flank, to attack in flank while I attacked in the rear. It was the homes of the men of my brigade that were being given to the flames by Sheridan, and the fierceness of their attack showed me the bitterness of their hatred of the wretches who were thus destroying their homes. I attacked in rear and flank and the enemy was broken, scattered, and pursued for several miles, indeed until the darkness of night proclaimed a truce.[6]

Sheridan's Torch

In this affair I captured several hundred head of cattle and sheep which had been taken from the farmers, also several wagons and teams and nine traveling forges. We took few prisoners but killed a greater percentage than I ever saw slain in an engagement of like duration. The soldiers who were required by General Sheridan to lay waste the beautiful Shenandoah Valley with the torch were brave, good men and were blameless in the part they took, for they only did as they were ordered. Every prisoner seemed heartily ashamed that such cowardly means had been employed in the endeavor to crush a brave people who never declined battle, and who could at all times have been met on the field under the rules of civilized war. Sheridan was retreating from an army under General Early much inferior to his own in numbers and equipment, and this wholesale destruction of property was not a military necessity, and Sheridan's boast, "that a crow could not fly over the without carrying its rations," in the track of his torch was a shameless admission of his cruelty.

Still in Pursuit

After getting into bivouac for the night I again wrote General Early informing him of the situation at that time and of my affair with the enemy that afternoon. I asked him if there was any change to be made in the program laid out for me, to which he replied that my instructions had already been given me, and he added that he desired me to hurry on to Winchester and damage the enemy all I could, for he was certain that the enemy "was leaving the valley." On the morning of the 8th I resumed pursuit, but there was no road by which I could pass the enemy and go on to Winchester, for he occupied them all, and the only way to comply with General Early's order was to drive the enemy out of my road. I overtook the rear of the cavalry column under Custer about midnight, and a running fight was kept up till late in the afternoon, when he drew off toward the pike and joined the main body of Sheridan's army. I could see no particular reason why I should go on to Winchester, yet my instructions were perfectly clear, and that point has been repeatedly fixed upon by General Early as my objective point, and regardless of Sheridan's position I had to go to Winchester. After Custer withdrew from the back road and that avenue was opened to Winchester, I moved [north] in the direction of that place, several miles, and might have gone all night had my scouts not reported the enemy at a halt at Strasburg, and a large body of cavalry moving from the pike to the back road in my rear with the evident purpose of cutting me off. I hastened back on receipt of the information and was just in time to strike the head of the enemy's column at Tom's Brook which I drove back by a vigorous sabre charge, and then withdrew across Tom's Brook to a high position where I bivouacked for the night.[7]

BATTLE AT TOM'S BROOK
A Fight in Which General Custer Won for the Shortcomings of a Colonel

The enemy spent the night immediately opposite me on the other side of the brook, and our pickets sat in their saddles within two hundred yards of each other all night. It was now very certain that I should be compelled to retreat before daylight or fight a force greatly superior to my own in the morning. Under my instructions I would not have dared to retreat and as fight was the only thing I could do I prepared for battle. I had my command in the saddle at daylight. I placed the "Laurel Brigade" in front, covered by mounted skirmishers, and held Payne's and Munford's Brigades in column close in the rear ready for immediate use. The battery of artillery under Captain [John W.] "Tuck" Carter, one of the bravest of the brave, was unlimbered in a favorable position and everything was put in order to receive the enemy, who was evidently moving upon us.

Custer's Charge

With my field glasses I easily recognized Custer as he rode along in front of his line and he evidently recognized me about the same time, for he wheeled his horse around facing me and galantly raised his hat and made me a profound bow, which I returned, as the men sent up a deafening cheer. Then, as his bugles sounded the charge, on came his dark battalions with the fury of a mighty cyclone. White's Battalion, which had been deployed as skirmishers, was rallied and formed on my right and front by its cool-headed, sagacious and gallant commander and as soon as the head of Custer's advancing column arrived on a line with him, White charged into him with his battalion with an intrepidity which could only have been impaired by utter contempt for his adversary and a perfect confidence in his own irresistibility and prowess. The shock of

White's Battalion was wonderful. The enemy staggered and before he could recover the "Laurel Brigade" was hurled upon him and sent him back across the brook.

A More Cautious Advance

Custer rallied and came back, but this time more cautiously; he deployed his mounted riflemen and advanced them in front of his cavalry. These were soon checked by my dismounted sharp-shooters and artillery, but the country was open and consequently most favorable to the enemy, whose force was much larger than my own. Finding my front so well guarded, large flanking columns were pushed out, which soon attacked my flanks, and even threatened my rear. I was compelled to retire, which by withdrawing one brigade at a time I was succeeding very well until the misbehavior of one of the colonels on Munford's brigade, when I lost a strong position in the rear to which I was retiring, with a view of making a stand there. Failing to find this regiment in the position it was ordered to take (behind a stone wall), I failed to check the enemy at this point and my command was badly broken up and driven in confusion for about two miles, when I rallied, and, taking a portion of the command moved back and attacked the enemy; but my force was too feeble to make much impression on him and I withdrew about three miles farther and took position at Columbia Furnace, from which the enemy made no effort to dislodge me.

Losses in Battle

In this engagement I lost my battery of artillery, but I did not much regret it, for I sold it for an excellent price. It was captured while pouring canister into the enemy, and for the sake of performing such service one can afford to throw away artillery. Many a battle was lost in this war by timid generals who were afraid of losing their artillery and consequently did not expose it to capture. I believe in pushing artillery to the front and using it freely, and if you lose it console yourself with the thought that you could well afford to. And if it was captured fighting you can rest assured that its captors paid dearly for it.

My loss in killed and wounded in this battle was heavy, but I lost but few prisoners. Among the killed was Captain Walk of my staff. He was a modest, retiring gentleman and a brave and efficient officer. Among the wounded was Lt. Col. M. D. Ball, of the Eleventh, and Major John W. Emmert, of my staff. Col. Ball's wounds healed in a few weeks sufficiently to enable him to return to his command, but Major Emmert was less fortunate, having been shot through the ankle. He was disabled for life. He did not return to the field again during the war, and being deprived of his valuable services midst the trying events which crowded upon us during the last scenes of this awful tragedy, was a great loss to me.[8]

General Early's Mistake

This fight at Tom's Brook was the only one I ever lost and was the first time the "Laurel Brigade" had ever sustained or shared defeat, and of course we were all very sore about it. I wrote General Early at once what had happened and chided him for pressing me on the heels of a force so far superior to my own in numbers and equipment, while he remained twenty-five miles in the rear with his infantry, and he replied comforting me with assurances of his confidence, and related how much worse his other cavalry division had suffered than mine had. Here was General Early's great mistake. He had two divisions of cavalry under him and each operated completely independent of the other. I was the junior officer and should have reported to Lomax; yet Lomax and I were fighting within three or four miles of each other and there was no communication between us. General Early, our "chief of cavalry," was twenty-five miles away.

The Misbehaving Colonel

Charges were preferred against the misbehaving colonel and he was tried by a court-martial and ably defended, but was dismissed from the service of the Confederate States. His offense was disobedience of orders and for leaving the field and his regiment during the battle and remaining absent from his command for twenty-four hours. The regiment commanded by this colonel was one of the best in the service and if it had been ably commanded on this occasion I believe I should not have lost my artillery. After this affair at Tom's Brook I increased my vigilance and prayed for an opportunity to pay the enemy back and when I heard that Custer had selected a camp for his division a few miles from the main body of Sheridan's army, I felt that my opportunity had come.

Scooping the Enemy

Therefore, on the night of the 17th of October, only eight days after the fight at Tom's Brook, I took [Brigadier] General [Bryan] Grimes' brigade of infantry and mounted it behind the cavalry of my division and by blind mountain paths moved around to the rear of the reported position of Custer (the old forge). I succeeded in gaining the position from which I intended making the attack unobserved, and I felt quit sure of success and in fancy had Custer and his division as my prisoners; but when I "scooped the enemy up," to my disgust I found that I had only captured a large picket reserve, Custer having moved back nearer the main body of

Sheridan's army. This raid of mine gave them such a scare that they allowed me no detached encampments after this. Failing in this raid on Custer, my command was much disappointed, especially the infantry, who had never participated in a cavalry raid before and they had endured great discomfort in riding bareback all night upon the poor horses that could carry only one rider safely. But these infantry boys felt they should be paid by someone for the trip, consequently they invariably robbed the man before them by taking his socks, handkerchiefs, corn cakes, and such other articles as he usually carried in his saddle pockets.

General Early held a council of war on the afternoon of the 18th [November 1864], and it was agreed that a general attack should be made on the enemy on the morning of the 19th. General Lomax was not at this meeting, and I was ordered to mass my division during the night of the 18th on the back road, to send Payne's Brigade to report to General Early, and with the other two brigades attack the enemy on Cedar Creek at 4:30 A.M., sharp. This was intended as a diversion for [Brigadier General J. B.] Gordon, who was to make the main attack on the other flank at 4 A.M. In case I succeeded penetrating the enemy's line I was directed to move on to New Town, on the pike, where I was told by General Early that Lomax would join me. The two brigades with which I was to operate, Wickham's and the Laurel Brigade, were commanded respectively by Colonel [Thomas H.] Owen, of the Third [Virginia Cavalry], and Colonel [Oliver R.] Funsten, of the Eleventh [Virginia Cavalry]. I attacked promptly as ordered, but I found the enemy well guarded on this flank, this being the direction from which an attack was expected, and with my small force I could make very little impression. I attacked with one brigade under Owen, dismounted, but the enemy was in the woods and on the alert, and after some hard fighting I was repulsed and fell back across Cedar Creek, but I kept the firing up until daylight, when I made a successful crossing, driving the brigade of cavalry from its position and pursuing it to within a mile and sight of New Town.

The Wrong Kind of Work

The fight between the main bodies was then going on in earnest and if I had been instructed to attack the enemy then flying before Gordon, I could have done great execution upon their broken ranks. As it was, I was simply pressing an organized and superior force of cavalry which did not appear to know what was going on. Indeed, General Early should have allowed me to have taken all my cavalry down the pike with his reserves, so that in case of Gordon's success I could have given the broken masses the sabre.

This I asked to be allowed to do, but it seemed best in the eyes of the lieutenant general to plan differently and he paid dearly for the mistake, for had I thrown my three brigades on the enemy after Gordon did break them I should have made it impossible for them ever to have rallied, or if I had failed in this, I could certainly have protected Early's flying and routed army from Sheridan's cavalry in the afternoon. As it was, I spent the day in skirmishing with the cavalry, which was strong enough at any time to have fallen upon me and crushed me for which I was not strong enough to drive off, so that I could attack the transportation wagons, which were stampeded and scattered along the pike for miles.

VICTORY THROWN AWAY
The Early Successes at Cedar Creek
Turned into Utter Defeat

As soon as Early's attack fagged, the enemy began to reorganize and from my position I could clearly see that he was preparing to renew the fight and so informed General Early. These evidences becoming so apparent I not only notified General Early, but reported the facts to General Gordon, who joined me in bringing these alarming facts to the notice of the commanding general. The enemy had been badly broken up in the early morning and had been pursued several miles, losing his camps and leaving his killed and wounded in our hands. Then, in the midst of victory, General Early suddenly halted and the enemy finding that he was not pursued also halted. As soon as this was done and time given to sum up the losses and take account of what was on hand for business it was quite apparent to the Federal commander that he was strong enough to go back and renew the contest.[9]

The Counterattack

Nothing was heard of Lomax and nothing was required of me by General Early except now and then, in answer to my warnings concerning the intentions of the enemy, to take care of myself. Consequently about 4 o'clock in the afternoon I sent one of my little brigades with a section of artillery, back to the south side of Cedar Creek to act as a base upon which I could retire in case of emergency. It was lucky for me that I did, for soon the enemy came down upon us all along the line and General Early and his little army were brushed out of the way and scattered like forest leaves before a mighty cyclone. I was hurried back faster than it becomes the dignity of troops to retreat until my artillery and sharpshooters, already in position at the creek, were able to strike the ranks of my pursuers, and then I was allowed to quietly take my position along the heights and to hold it unmolested.

Early's Defeated Army

I sent our scouts to learn where General Early was as soon as it was dark, and to my horror and amazement, the enemy was found all along the pike from Cedar Creek to Fisher's Hill; but General Early was not to be found, nor could I hear anything more than that he had been routed and was fleeing up the valley. It was now ten o'clock at night, and that I might be in position of safety I began to retire up the valley, when I was joined by one of General Early's staff officers, who informed me that General Early was at Fisher's Hill and wished me to move everything I had to that point as quickly as possible. I directed Colonel Funsten to move the command to Fisher's Hill and I rode rapidly with General Early's aide to the position where he had just left the general. I found General Early, General Gordon, and General [John] Pegram on the pike on the summit of Fisher's Hill and from them learned the sad fate of the army—that army which had in the morning achieved one of the most remarkable victories recorded in the annals of war, at the close of the day had suffered an unprecedented and shameful defeat. General Early displayed great strategic skill in planning this attack upon Sheridan's army, which was not only strongly fortified and occupied a strong position naturally, but was vastly superior to his own in numbers and equipment. Early's plans were bold and masterly and equal in brilliance to anything conceived by the minds of our great generals, but as a tactician he was greatly at fault. All whoever served with General Early could not have failed to notice how deficient he was in knowledge of topography of the "coup d'oeil" [a rapid glance] on the battlefield. He never appeared to understand the ground or the location of roads upon his maps, and would never believe the statements of his scouts; and worst of all, as it so happened that the greater portion of the adversary's army was cavalry, he had no idea of managing cavalry and had very little respect for its efficiency and a low estimate of its value. Yet, after all, it was cavalry that destroyed him.

The Line on Stony Creek

I left Colonel Owen with a strong detachment on the back road, and put Funsten's Brigade in the Fisher's Hill trenches, and held Payne in the saddle for emergencies, and General Early, with the remnant of his army, resumed his march up the valley before daylight. There was no effort made by Sheridan to pursue us and really he did not appear to realize the completeness of his victory. If he had pursued vigorously on the morning of the 20th, he could have galloped over every obstruction we could have thrown in his path and could have captured Early and his army. I remained in the works at Fisher's Hill till the sun was well up in the morning, then sent General Payne, with his brigade, back to Edenburg, with instructions to pick up all stragglers and get in position on the south side of Stony Creek, where he could aid me in the event of my being hotly pursued by the enemy, but the enemy did not pursue; there was a little fog early in the morning, which soon cleared off, and I think it must have been as late as 10 o'clock when the last of my cavalry rode off from the hill. The enemy came on after us slowly, but when he came in sight of us at Edenburg, he halted and a few shots turned him back. I left a picket at Edenburg, and proceeded up the valley about three miles and encamped for the night. General Early established his headquarters at New Market and I held the line at Stony Creek with the cavalry.

Early in November, Sheridan gave up the line of Cedar Creek and moved down [north] toward Winchester, and as soon as this fact was reported to General Early, the plucky old soul picked up his little army and started after him with as much confidence as if he had an army big enough to whip him. Moving along down the valley in advance of General Early I encountered on the 11th [November 1864] a brigade on the middle road to New Town, which I at once attacked and drove off in the direction of Kearnstown and, pursuing, I came upon a large force of the enemy's infantry on the Opequon. Not strong enough to attempt to dislodge this force, I deployed dismounted sharpshooters and kept up a pretty lively skirmish till night and then bivouacked for the night within range of the enemy's guns. Early on the morning of the 12th my pickets on the back road were driven in, but Colonel Funsten, who was supporting this portion of the line with the Laurel Brigade, gallantly reestablished his line and charged and drove the enemy several miles, capturing a number of prisoners, both horses and arms. This dash of Funsten aroused Custer, who followed Funsten back with his entire division, and overtaking him just as he was going into camp, charged him, but the gallant little brigade turned upon him and a very desperate struggle ensued in which the Laurel Brigade lost heavily; but Custer was held at bay until I got notice of what was going on. Then I moved across with Munford's (Wickham's) Brigade, then commanded by Colonel Morgan, and struck the enemy in flank and sent him back down the valley in a hurry, capturing several score of prisoners and recapturing such of our own as had fallen into enemy hands during his temporary success.

In this skirmish we lost one of the finest soldiers in our service and one of the noblest spirits even born, Colonel Thomas Marshall, of the Seventh Virginia Cavalry. He fell while leading the gallant, old Seventh to victory. It was just the death he would have courted had he then known that the new-born Confederacy, the pride of his life, was doomed to die in the arms of General Robert E. Lee six months hence at Appomattox! Indeed, had that event been foreseen by our entire army there would have been but few to witness the apple-tree scene at Appomattox, and the torch lit by Sheridan in the valley would have been carried to the homes of those who applauded the act on the other side of the Susquehanna.[10]

Winter Hardships Begun

Finding the enemy too strongly posted on the Opequon, General Early concluded not to risk and attack upon him there, and on the morning of the 13th he retired up the valley unpursued and re-established his camp at New Market. Winter was upon us, forage for our poor horses was extremely scarce, and rations were scant, and all this in the midst of the ruin and desolation which Sheridan's fires had produced, rendered our condition a gloomy one, indeed. On the 20th of November my quartermaster informed me that it would be impossible for him to feed my horses longer than one week. The distance to which he had to send for supplies was so great that the animals were barely able to haul their own rations for the round trip. The situation was desperate and immediate remedy was necessary.

THE AFFAIR AT NEW CREEK
A Successful Raid in Search of Food
A Pleasing Little Victory

My scouts had reported supplies in abundance in the valley of the South Branch of the Potomac, and I, therefore, proposed to General Early to let me go there with my command in search of food, and obtaining his consent, I arranged to have my quartermaster and commissary take everything upon wheels that could carry a ration and accompany me, and on the 26th of November [1864] I took Payne's and Funston's Brigades and started. Moving directly across the mountains through Brock's Gap, I reached Moorefield about 1 P.M. on the 27th. Not wishing the presence of my command to be known until I had looked over the situation, I ordered the column to halt upon the fork and I rode into the town with only one or two guides. I had been in town only a few minutes when I was informed that the enemy was approaching the place from the direction of New Creek.

A Quick Capture

I rode to a high point where I could see the force and estimate its strength, and seeing that it numbered only a few hundred men I sent hurriedly to the rear for a regiment. Only McNeill's squadron of irregular cavalry and Company F, of the Seventh Virginia Cavalry, were at hand and these I sent by an obscure road to the rear of the enemy and ordered up the command at a trot; but before I could get the troops to attack in front, McNeill had attacked in the rear and captured nearly every man, together with their only piece of artillery. I had previously intended to make a dash at New Creek, after taking in the supplies on the Branch and Patterson's Creek, but as a few stragglers had escaped from the detachment just captured, I was afraid they would return to their friends and report my presence, therefore I determined to go on that night, so as to reach New Creek in advance of the fugitives.

Capture of Fort Kelly

Rations in abundance were found at Moorfield, and as soon as all were well fed I resumed the march, continuing all night until I came within sight of the enemy's pickets about 9 A.M. on the morning of the 28th. It was a bright and beautiful day. These pickets knew that their friends had gone out a day or two before in the direction whence I was approaching and my appearance did not seem to disturb them. I moved leisurely onto them as though I was on the most amicable terms of peace with them and they did not discover their mistake until they were pounced upon by my provost guards and made prisoners; then it was too late to warn their friends, who had confided their safety to their vigilant keeping. After the advance pickets were taken in without giving the alarm, we rode on the reserves in the same way and picked them up, and finally I rode with my whole command right up and under the guns of Fort Kelly, dashing into this strongly fortified citadel and capturing the entire garrison with the loss of two men killed and three wounded. My killed and wounded, I think, suffered from the reckless firing of my own men.

Work at New Creek

I captured 800 prisoners at New Creek, a large number of horses and mules, and eight stand of colors. I loaded up and brought off a large quantity of commissary supplies and destroyed a vast amount of commissary, quartermaster, and ordnance stores. I cut down and spiked the four heavy siege guns in Fort Kelly and brought off four beautiful field pieces with their limbers and caissons. While I was destroying the government supplies at New Creek I sent Major McDonald, commanding the Eleventh Virginia Cavalry, to Piedmont, where he drove off the guard and destroyed a great deal of public property. As soon as McDonald returned to me at New Creek I gathered up all the supplies that could be taken with us and started for home.[11]

I knew that my presence in West Virginia would be reported to Sheridan and that he would make an effort to intercept me on my way back; therefore I sent one regiment ahead to hold the narrow pass between Petersburg and Moorefield and changed my route for returning by the way of Petersburg instead of Moorefield, and sure enough, my regiment got to the gap about a half hour before Custer appeared and thus cut off his little "cutting off" game. I marched leisurely back to the valley, after gathering up all the beeves and fat sheep found on the line of march, all of which I safely delivered to the commissariat of General Early's starving army.

My command returned from this trip to the enemy's country very much improved, for after the capture of New Creek, I moved slowly back to the valley, halting several days at Petersburg, in the midst of plenty; therefore, the condition of my horses was greatly benefited. The moral condition of my command was also greatly elevated by this successful dash into the enemy's country, and many men who were absent looking for fresh horses or from sickness hurried back to avoid criticism or to be certain of participating in the next expedition of like character.

AT LACY'S SPRING
Custer Caught Napping and How Certain
Hard Knocks Awake Him

On the 20th of December my scouts reported a division of the enemy's cavalry moving up the valley, and I at once assembled my little command and moved down to meet him. I reached Harrisonburg late on the night of the 22nd and learned that the enemy, consisting of Custer's Division was encamped at Lacy's Spring, about nine miles distant. My scouts, who had been watching this body of enemy, agreed that its strength was at least 5,000 men, and as mine was less then 2,000 and there was no support nearby, I saw instantly that my safety demanded that I should attack him in his camp that night. I at once notified General Early by wire (using our secret cipher) of my purpose and obtained his consent, and at 1 A.M. on the morning of the 23rd I moved out from Harrisonburg, and by following blind roads I got up within a hundred yards of Custer's bivouac without encountering a picket.

A Successful Dash

As I rode up the enemy's numerous campfires presented in the cold, sleety nights a very beautiful appearance. The evening before there were several high fences, which I feared would seriously interfere with my night movements, but when I halted my command and rode ahead with General Payne, to reconnoiter the ground, I found that the enemy's campfires had consumed all the fences, and there was no obstacle of that kind to fear. We returned to our waiting troops; it had been raining and freezing all night and the clothes of my men were covered with ice, the ground was also a sheet of ice, and my horses were smooth and could scarcely stand up; but here we were in the immediate presence of the enemy, had come here to fight him, and there was no backing out. Plans were hastily made and without a yell or the sound of a bugle we swept down on the half-sleeping foe like an avalanche, and the result was all that I could have desired. If the enemy had all been encamped together I would have destroyed Custer's entire command, but they were so scattered that a large percentage were in their saddles before I could reach them. All that I struck were scattered and badly demoralized, and I am informed that Custer escaped from the farmhouse where he was spending the night before completing his toilet. In a few minutes the fun was all over, but in this short time we had some hard fighting. As soon, however, as Custer could extricate himself he retired back down the valley and not daring to follow him I returned to the valley, rejoicing at my good fortune in escaping a battle of Custer's planning.[12]

To Gordonsville and Back

Returning up the valley I was met by a staff officer for General Early, informing me that a large body of the enemy's cavalry was moving upon Gordonsville and directing me to move as rapidly as possible to that place in support of General Fitz Lee, who was assembling his scattered troops at that point to meet the enemy. I accordingly turned off and pushed through Rock Fish Gap, and by marching all night reached Gordonsville at noon on the 24th. I was rejoiced to learn on my arrival that General Lomax had repulsed the enemy a few hours before and all was then quiet and the enemy had gone back. I then leisurely marched back to Swope's Depot and reoccupied my camp.

A Plan to Go to Beverly

Winter had now set in earnest, the ground was covered with snow, and the weather was very cold. The few rations collected on my New Creek expedition were now about exhausted, and no one could tell where the next rations were to come from. My scouts had reported that there was a quantity of the enemy's supplies at a little place in the mountains called Beverly, and that there was only a thousand or so inexperienced troops guarding them. I reported my condition to General Early and asked permission to go to Beverly and collect there all I could and thus keep my command together as long as possible. But the distance to Beverly was so great [deep in the central part of West Virginia, about 50 miles from Buchanan] and the uncertainty of success after I got there decided him against it and he refused to allow me to go. My condition was desperate, my horses were starving, and my men were not half fed, and when General R. E. Lee summoned General Early to a conference at Petersburg and left Fitz Lee in command of the valley I took my petition to this gallant little soldier and he at once said "go!"

A Gallant Three Hundred

After I had obtained authority for going I found it difficult to muster enough serviceable horses to mount a serviceable regiment. Colonel Tom Munford reported his brigade unfit for duty, and I called upon the Laurel Brigade and that of General Payne for volunteers, and to this appeal all the privates responded from all the brigades. They were willing to go on foot, or any way, but I succeeded in finding 300 horses able to make the journey, and those I mounted and divided into two detachments of 150 men each, one under Colonel Morgan of the First Virginia and the other under the command of Colonel Cook of the Eighth Virginia, and I can safely say that a more intelligent, more gallant and more reliable three hundred that composed my little army of invasion was never assembled in one command.

CAPTURE OF BEVERLY
Some Adventures in the Mountains with
Winter Blasts Blowing Shrilly

I left camp with my 300 on the morning of the 7th of February [1865], marched through Buffalo Gap and proceeded via the Parkersburg Turnpike. The region into which I soon passed was entirely abandoned; it had been the theater of war in the early part of the contest and its inhabitants had abandoned it. The snow was deep and the road was unbroken; not a single track had disturbed the snow since its fall in early winter. I reached Jackson's River; it was full and the ice was running rapidly. I crossed it with great difficulty, losing one horse and nearly drowning one man. General Early, returning to the valley, heard I had gone on the forbidden exhibition, sent a messenger to bring me back, but the dangerous appearance of Jackson's River turned him back and I was permitted to go on.[13]

Obstacles Overcome

I reached Tygart's River in Randolph County a short while after dark on the night of the 10th and found it very high and out of its banks, and of course, not fordable. My guides informed me that to reach Beverly I would be compelled to cross the river several times, and also that Beverly was on the same side of the river that I was at that time and that it was possible for me to reach it by a blind and rough mountain road without crossing the river. My position was now a desperate one. I had crossed the Cheat Mountain in a thunderstorm and my men were drenched in rain. As I came down the mountain into Tygart's Valley the temperature fell below freezing, and the rain turned into a cold, drifting snowstorm. The bridle path along the side of the mountain was tedious and I did not reach Beverly until 4 o'clock in the morning.

Capture of Beverly

I had passed entirely around the place, and coming up in the rear, I encountered no pickets, and I dismounted all my men except one squadron and marched them up to within fifty yards of the cabins in which my victims slept. I formed my line at right angle to the line of those cabins, and then rode along the line (I was still on crutches from my wounds at Nevellious), and cautioned every man as to how we should act; then raising a yell we dashed into the cantonment. It so happened that all the officers were off at a ball in the village, and the men, without anyone in command, were soon prisoners. The officers, learning of the attack upon their quarters, left the scenes of revelry and made an effort to reach their men, but Colonel Cook met them with his squadron and dispersed or captured them. In doing so this gallant officer received a wound in his knee which cost him the loss of his leg.

On the Way Back

As soon as it was daylight I collected such stores as were found in the village, and with the prisoners, whose numbers were more than three times the number of my entire force, I moved back towards home. I halted one day just outside of Beverly to allow the river to run down, and while I was lying there my surgeons amputated Colonel Cook's leg, and not knowing that they had not left the village, that night I withdrew my guard, and as soon as I did so several Federal officers came out from their hiding places and took my surgeons' horses and rode off. During the flight before light in the street such officers escaped Colonel Cook's cavalry when they ran into private houses and were concealed.

An Amusing Incident

There was a very amusing incident connected with myself, which I might as well relate. After the prisoners were all taken care of, and Colonel Morgan had collected all of his command and the Commissary and Quartermaster's Departments had collected all stores, I went into the house of a gentleman for breakfast. After breakfast, I went into a bedroom, the most quiet place I could find, to have my wound dressed. Here, my surgeon dressed my wound after which I laid down on the bed to rest for a short time, as I was tired and sleepy. As I was thus occupied a captain of the Federal army was hiding under the very bed I was laying on, and of course, as I did not know it he escaped capture and a hard march to Richmond. When I returned to my old camp at Swope's Depot I found that those I had left in camp had not been benefited by rest, and the old story of starvation was again heard.[14]

————————————————————————————

CHAPTER 5

IN SHERIDAN'S PATH
The Enemy Held at Mount Crawford
The Disaster to General Early

Fitz Lee moved Payne's and Munford's Brigades east of the Blue Ridge and the Laurel Brigade was left alone in the valley. This I kept together the best I could, and when Sheridan began his march up the valley I met him on the 28th of February at Mount Crawford with about 500 men. General Early was then at Staunton with a small force of infantry and artillery under General Whorton, and I endeavored to hold Sheridan at the North River, which was quite high, until General Early could get out of the way or get to some defensible position. I held the bridges and as the stream could not be readily forded I detained Sheridan at Mount Crawford for one day. The river had sufficiently receded to allow to ford it, and he crossed a large body of cavalry above the town and drove my small force away.

At Waynesboro

I retired to Staunton and when I reached that place on the night of March 1 [1865], I found that General Early and his little army had gone to Waynesboro. I then moved my force to Fishersville and rode on to see General Early. I found him in bed in Waynesboro on the morning of the 2nd of March. I related what had occurred and told him as nearly as I could what I believed the force under Sheridan was. I also gave him my opinion as to what I thought he ought to do, and do immediately. This was to get on the other side of the river. This precaution I believe he intended to take, but

Sheridan came too soon and he was caught off his guard and his little army was captured.

The Disaster to Early

At the close of my interview with General Early at Waynesboro I was directed by him to go back and get my little force together, and hang on the flank of the enemy and to damage him all I could. I did go back, and not long after I reached my men I heard the firing at Waynesboro. I sent a scout to watch the enemy, thinking, of course, that General Early would be found on the other side of the river in an impregnable position, and I laughed at the idea of Sheridan attacking him there. But soon my man returned and reported "another disaster," and before night I saw the long line of prisoners being led back to the rear by a detachment of 1,200 or 1,500 Federal cavalry. There was nothing now for me to do but to try and recapture these prisoners and I, therefore, followed along and watched my opportunity. I attacked the guard near Harrisonburg on the night of the 4th [March 1865] and enabled a few prisoners to escape, and as the Shenandoah was high I sent a detachment over the river to hold the fords and to detain the enemy in Meeny Bottoms, below Rude's Hill two days, and on the morning of the 7th I collected all the force I could and attacked him as he was crossing the river and caused him to abandon his artillery.[1]

ON SHERIDAN'S TRACK
From the Valley to Petersburg
The Battle of Five Forks

I then returned and followed Sheridan, who was moving down the James River toward Richmond, and breaking the James River and Kanawha Canal wherever he could. After passing Scottsville, Sheridan turned off and crossed the Pamunkey River in Hanover and marched via the White House, where he recrossed the Pamunkey and then marched across to Petersburg and joined Grant. While Sheridan was marching through Caroline and King William counties I reached Hanover County House on the 16th and found General Longstreet there with a portion of his corps. Sheridan was then near Magnolia Church on the north side of the river, and our plan was to cross the Pamunkey at Nelson's Ferry and throw ourselves in front of Sheridan to force him to fight if we could, but the pontoon train failed to reach us, and the bridge, which I had constructed of ferry boats and rafts, was not completed until the morning of the 17th, when the most of General Longstreet's corps crossed. Before anything could be done orders were received from General R. E. Lee recalling everything to Petersburg, and Sheridan was allowed to proceed without interruption.

I was directed to the extreme right of General Lee's army to take charge of the pickets and outposts in that direction and I established my camp at the Nottoway River, near Spencer's Mill; but I had been in camp only two days when I received orders to return to Dinwiddie Court House. The same order notifying me that Sheridan's cavalry was moving towards the same point, I called in all the pickets and in a few hours I was on the road to the point mentioned. The night was very dark and the recent rains had raised all the streams, and when I got near Dinwiddie Court House I found that I could not cross Stony Run and moved up to Scott's, where I forded the stream with much difficulty, swimming most of the horses, and to prevent the ammunition in the artillery chests from getting wet the boxes were unpacked and the cartridges were carried over by hand. This delayed me some, but I got around to the Baptist Church about 8 A.M. on the 31st of March [1865], where I found General Fitz Lee and General Pickett. I learned from them that Sheridan was at Dinwiddie Court House, which fact I would have discovered myself, and perhaps, to my sorrow, if I would have been permitted by the high water in Stony Run to have crossed and gone to the court house as ordered, instead of coming around as I did. However, I was ordered to prepare for battle, which would be made on the enemy at once.

The Plan of Attack

It was planned that I should take my division, then composed of the Laurel Brigade, under General James Dearing, and General McCausland's Brigade, and move by blind roads across to the Petersburg Plank Road, about three miles from Dinwiddie Court House, at a place called Hargrave's, and Fitz and Pickett were to move directly upon the court house. Fitz Lee had his own and W. H. F. Lee's Divisions and the horse artillery, and Pickett had five brigades of infantry and a battalion of artillery. Instead of moving immediately as I was first told, we did not move before 12 or 1 o'clock. Then I was instructed to follow W. H. F. Lee, and as soon as the enemy fell back, uncovering the road I was to take, I proceeded to carry out my original instructions, but when we reached Chambelain's Creek the enemy was found occupying it in force and in driving him off our whole command became engaged and the original plan for penetrating to the Plank Road was abandoned.

A Heavy Skirmish

The country was heavily wooded and the cavalry was dismounted and deployed on the right and left of the infantry, and the enemy was steadily driven back, but the engagement could not be considered more than a heavy skirmish, which lasted until after dark, during which time the enemy was driven about two miles. I was shot through the arm late in the afternoon and spent a feverish, restless night. It was understood when the firing ceased at night that hostilities would be resumed the next morning. I sent around and imparted this information to my pickets and my line was in position at daylight expecting orders to advance. None came, and about 8 o'clock in the morning of the first [April] I received orders from General Pickett to fall back to Five Forks. When I mounted and moved out to the road I found the infantry marching back in such haste that I drew out of the road and allowed them to pass, then followed on slowly to Five Forks, and was surprised that I was not pursued by the enemy.[2]

A Memorable Lunch

I found General Pickett at the forks, and as the country was heavily wooded I could see no opportunity for the use of cavalry. As I had been so long in the saddle, and my horses and men needed rest, I asked permission to move back about a mile in his rear on the other side of Hatcher's Run and removed saddles and feed. I had brought some excellent fresh shad from the Nottoway with me, and I invited General Pickett to go back and lunch with me. Not wishing to leave his command until he had seen all of his brigade in position he promised to join me in an hour, and at the appointed time he and General Fitz Lee returned to me.

Battle of Five Forks

While we were at lunch couriers came in from the officers commanding the pickets on the White Oak and other parallel roads, reporting the advance of the enemy. Some time was spent over lunch, and during which no firing was heard, and we concluded that the enemy was not in much of a hurry to find us at Five Forks. A courier sent by General Pickett from my position to Five Forks was fired on just over the creek, and came galloping back and reported the enemy in the road in front of us and just in the rear of our position at Five Forks! General Pickett ordered me to push a line of skirmishers over the creek and ascertain the truth of the matter. About this time the battle broke out along all the line at Five Forks. My skirmishers were driven back and the enemy appeared in large force in my front. General Pickett made an effort to join his command, which was then fighting in front of him, but failed, the enemy being between him and his command; he came riding back in a big hurry and called for the Dinwiddie Troop as guides. As soon as this company could be mounted he rode off again, but I think his troops were routed before he reached them.

The Battle of Five Forks was of short duration, but quite used up that portion of our army which was engaged in it. It seems to have been a surprise to General Pickett, yet one would have thought that he would have been on the alert in the presence of an enemy which he had so recently been fighting, but from all that I could see on the occasion I am satisfied that all the generalship and management were on the Federal side.[3]

THE GREAT RETREAT BEGINS
Abandonment of Petersburg—Brushes with the Enemy on the Road

I remained in position on the Ford's Road, where I was during the fight at Five Forks, all night, and General Fitz Lee remained with me. About 9 A.M. on the 2nd [April], I was ordered to withdraw and follow the command of General [George T.] Anderson's [Brigade] who was moving from Petersburg, which was being abandoned, up the Appomattox River in the direction of Amelia Court House. I was being closely pressed by the enemy when ordered to withdraw, and it was no easy matter to obey the order. I mounted General Dearing's Brigade and then withdrew General McCausland on foot, and by supporting him with the mounted men he was soon able to pass to Dearing's rear and mount his men. When in the saddle I rode off in the direction General Anderson had taken and was soon out of the reach of the enemy's infantry and his cavalry, being only in small force, did not dare to press me. Near Trinity Church I found General Fitz Lee with his division, and as he there took the position of rear guard, I moved on until I overtook the rear of General Anderson's column. This was moving into position near Perkinson's house and was under the command of General Bushrod Johnson.[4]

Waiting for Cooke

General Johnson informed me that he had been ordered to wait there for General Cooke, who was supposed to be marching on the Namozine Road, in the direction of Mount Pleasant Church. As soon as his line was formed I took position on the left, and soon General Fitz Lee came up and took position on my left. This position we held all afternoon and could hear nothing of General Cooke. The enemy came in front of us just before night and opened a light fire on us, which we returned, and this was kept up until 12 o'clock that night. When nothing was heard from Cooke we resumed our march in the direction of Namozine Church until we crossed the creek, then we halted and rested until daylight.

The Rear Guard

When the march was resumed on the morning of the 3rd I was in command of the rear guard, and kept up a continued skirmish with the enemy. When reaching Namozine Church I was relieved of rear guard duty by the command of General W. H. F. Lee, but the enemy pressed him so vigorously that he left the main road, and the enemy came galloping upon me before I knew that General Lee had gone. Fortunately the enemy was very much scattered or thinned out when he came on me and when I wheeled about and charged him I was able to strike him a crippling blow, which caused him to proceed more cautiously the remainder of the day. This dash of the enemy upon my rear induced General Anderson to leave Colonel [William B.] Tabb's [59th Virginia] Regiment of infantry of Wise's Brigade, in the rear with me, and we retired slowly in the direction of Tabernacle Church, the enemy keeping a respectful distance.[5]

At Deep Creek Bridge

Fearing the enemy would pass our flank and cut us off from Deep Creek Bridge, which was our only crossing, I was ordered to send a regiment forward to occupy and hold the bridge. This regiment met the enemy about a mile from the bridge and was driven back. I then pushed to the front with my division, and aided by the venerable old statesman and gallant soldier, General Henry A. Wise, we drove the enemy off handsomely, killing and wounding a number and capturing thirty prisoners. After crossing Deep Creek we halted for the night at Tabernacle Church, and the cavalry, which had again gotten together, held the line of defense during the night. Fitz Lee on the right, I in the center, and W. H. F. Lee on the left.

The Stand at the Creek

We destroyed the bridge and as the creek was not easily forded we made it a serious obstacle to the enemy. Several efforts to force a crossing early on the morning of the 4th were gallantly repulsed by the Eleventh Regiment, under Colonel M. D. Ball, and the Twelfth under Major [John L.] Knott. About 9 o'clock the enemy came up in force and crossed the creek on foot on the right and the left of me, and I was forced to retire. General Fitz Lee was directed to move back to the Devil's Bridge Road and cover the rear of the wagon trains belonging to the main force under General Robert E. Lee, which had crossed to the right bank of the Appomattox River.

A FIGHT NEAR AMELIA
The Gallantry of General Dearing's Men in an
Affair at the Springs

I found on reaching the wagon train that it was very much scattered, and to protect it I took position near the Pleasant Oaks, after which Lieutenant General Anderson posted his corps on my right, and the threatening attitude of the enemy kept us in line all night, though nothing more than skirmishing at long range occurred. On the morning of the 5th I moved to Amelia Court House and saw nothing of the enemy. My command, men and horses, were suffering for food, and as I had been informed that rations would be issued at Amelia Court House I halted there and endeavored to find them, but only a little cornmeal could be procured. There was nothing for the horses, but before I had given up the search for food an order came from General R. E. Lee directing me to move at once to Amelia Springs and drive the enemy's cavalry which was in that vicinity burning our wagons.

Amelia Springs

I mounted at once and proceeded at a trot and soon reached Shank's farm, where the wagons had been burned and learned that the enemy had disappeared. General Fitz Lee, with his division, had gone toward Painesville, and Major Ryles of Fitz Lee's staff was left behind to direct me to Amelia Springs. Just before reaching the springs I came upon what I took to be a brigade of the enemy's cavalry drawn up in front of me on a high ridge. Without waiting to see what his intentions were I ordered General Dearing to "ride over'em!" And the words were scarcely out of my mouth before he waved his hat over his head and commanded "Forward! Gallop! March!" And in a moment he had closed with the enemy, broke his line and sent him thundering on through Amelia Springs, Dearing and his gallant riders close on their heels. Passing up the hill near Jeter's house the enemy were so closely pursued that they left the road and turned in disorder to the right and escaped through the pines and escaped.

Captain McGuire's Charge

In advance of Dearing's column was Captain Hugh McGuire, of the Eleventh Virginia. When he saw the enemy scatter through the woods so as to elude pursuit, he halted the advancing troops and began to reorganize them so as to be ready for a forward movement when the troops had all closed up, when fresh troops coming out from Jetersville to aid those who had just been beaten, came suddenly and unexpectedly upon McGuire; but as quickly as though the gallant captain ordered the charge and at the enemy he went, and although their numbers were six times his own, the fury of his attack was more than they could withstand. The enemy was again broken and chased at a run into Jetersville, where the infantry was met in large force and I withdrew the cavalry back to the springs.

McGuire and Rutherford

In the last spirited charge the gallant Captain McGuire received a fatal wound from which he died in a few days, and Captain [James]

Rutherford, of General Dearing's staff, was also killed. These were two unusually promising men and promising soldiers. In this race we captured about a hundred prisoners, and among them a courier bearing valuable communications to General Meade, the receipt of which was of great service to General R. E. Lee, to whom they were immediately forwarded. I was up most of the night trying to get some rations for the men and forage for my horses. There were a great many of my wounded in the bivouac, and these had to be cared for, and these cares kept me on my feet all night.[6]

An Incident on the Road

Early on the morning of the 6th I was ordered to move to Rice's Station, on the South Side Railroad, and report to Lieutenant General Longstreet. I procured a guide and pushed on through the fields and blind roads, so as to avoid the crowded roads upon which the infantry and artillery were marching, and thus I reached the station in advance of General Longstreet. Just before I reached the station, however, my guide lost his way and I had to impress an old farmer, through whose yard I was passing, to help us out of our difficulty. I had noticed that the old man was standing among his slaves as I rode up, and when I told him he must get his horse and go with us, he protested lustily and said that to do so would ruin him; that he was "selling his slaves, little and big, to the Georgians for $25 a head in gold," and if I interfered with him, "the Yankees would soon have them all and I would get nothing!" I don't know where the Georgians got so much gold, but I could not doubt the old gentleman's statement, for his manner was too earnest and candid to be mistaken. When I assured him that I only required him for a little while he hurried off for his home and I was soon safely conducted through the brush to the station.

DEATH OF DEARING
The Fierce Clash at Watson's Farm
Where Some True Hero's Fell

When I reached Rice's Station I learned that an infantry and cavalry force, numbering about twelve or fifteen hundred, had earlier gone up the road towards the high bridge. I at once applied to General Longstreet for permission to follow and destroy these troops, which had evidently been sent to destroy the high bridge. After establishing sufficient pickets and leaving one regiment behind to support them, I was permitted to move on in pursuit of this party. My command, composed of portions of my own and Fitz Lee's Division, numbered in all about fifteen hundred men. I overtook the enemy at about 1 o'clock near Watson's farm. It had been raining and the sky was still overcast and the air was foggy and thick. The enemy had received notice of my approach and had posted his infantry in a strong position along the line of a heavy oak forest and behind a high fence. The cavalry was not in sight when I came up.

Dearing and Washburne

I dismounted Fitz Lee's Division under command of Colonel Munford and moved it through the dense pines unobserved by the enemy. Immediately in front of and facing the line the enemy had formed, and with Dearing commanding my division in the saddle, he charged the enemy in flank. General Reid, the adjutant of the Army of the James, was in command, and a Colonel [Francis] Washburne was commanding the cavalry. As soon as Dearing moved out so as to threaten Reid's flank, Colonel Washburne charged him with his cavalry and I never witnessed a more handsome attack than he at this time led. Dearing met him with the same undaunted, determined pluck and the most savage hand-to-hand fight I ever witnessed was the result. Dearing and Washburne were both killed within a few feet of each other. Whether they had slain each other I cannot say, but many think they did. Colonel Boston and Major Thompson were also killed in this cavalry fight and every man in Washburne's command was killed, wounded or captured; none tried to escape.

Breathed's Fight for Life

I was unable, from a wound received through my left arm at Five Forks a few days before, to use my sabre, but during the fight I rode among my men and encouraged them by my presence, which was all I could do. While I looked on I saw Major James Breathed, of the horse artillery, attack two Federal captains, Breathed with pistol, and the Federals with sabers. They closed before Breathed had an opportunity to shoot, or if he shot he missed his mark, and when I saw him the Federals were cutting and striking at him with their sabers while Breathed was exceedingly busy warding them off with his pistol. Their horses were run against Breathed's and he was finally knocked off his horse, and in falling his foot was caught between his horse and one of the Federal captains, pulling off one of his boots. Breathed then shot and killed one of the officers and Courier Scruggs dashed out from my side and killed the other. In a moment Breathed was back in the saddle again, with only one boot, and again joined in the fight.

Lives Thrown Away

As soon as the cavalry was disposed of, the infantry in the woods was charged and driven back through the woods, where they raised a white flag and surrendered. In this fight, in the woods,

General Reid, commanding the Federals, was killed and Major Knott of the Twelfth Virginia Cavalry, on our side, was also killed. My loss in this fight was very heavy. As the end was so near, it would have been better to have allowed the enemy to capture us all and burn all the bridges in the country rather than to have thrown away such lives as Dearing's, Boston's, Thompson's, and Knott's, for they died for no purpose...the cause was already lost! The prisoners, arms, ambulances and horses were turned over to General Longstreet's proper officers and I moved back to Rice's Station and took my position on the right of General Longstreet's line, and made all the necessary arrangements and preparations to meet the enemy, who was then reported moving upon us from the "junction."[7]

STILL WESTWARD MARCHING
Gregg Struck Hard on the Cumberland Plank Road
Grant's Trains

Night came without a battle, but we spent the night in line, expecting a battle at daylight. When the anxious night passed the enemy was found to have left our rear and our retreat was resumed. I having been joined by Fitz Lee, the cavalry retired in the direction of Farmville, all under Fitz Lee's command. The enemy pursued us slowly and nothing more than skirmishing at long range was engaged in so far as the cavalry was concerned until we reached Farmville. At this point the enemy rushed on us and endeavored to prevent us from crossing the Appomattox River, and in this he partially succeeded, but my division, which was cut off from the bridge, moved up the river about two miles and forded, while Fitz Lee's Division crossed on the bridge of the Cumberland Court House Road.[8]

On the Cumberland Plank Road

After I crossed the river I marched down its left bank to join Fitz Lee from whom I had been separated. When I reached the Cumberland Plank Road I found Fitz Lee's Division under the command of Colonel Munford (Fitz Lee being temporarily absent), making vigorous preparations to meet the enemy who was reported to be approaching from Farmville and supposedly very near, but the country being very wooded he was not yet in sight. I had ridden a little ahead of my division, and as I was the ranking officer I gave Colonel Munford some hasty instructions and rode rapidly back to put my division in proper place to participate in the defense of the position Colonel Munford was required to hold. Our entire transportation was moving upon roads parallel to the Appomattox River and just in rear of the line Colonel Munford had selected for the defense of them. These wagons had recrossed to the north side of the Appomattox below Farmville and were moving in the direction of Lynchburg.

Attack and Repulse

My division was marching upon an obscure road at right angles to the road the enemy was moving on and as I rode back to meet it I saw the enemy deploy his line and move up to attack Munford. I hurried the Laurel Brigade under Colonel White at a trot and upon coming in sight of the enemy he charged him handsomely. The enemy, in the meantime, having dislodged Munford, was much scattered among the wagons and my attack with White, followed instantly by McCausland was a complete surprise to them and he was badly broken up, losing many prisoners, among them General Gregg, who was in command, and otherwise suffering greatly. He hastily retreated in the direction he had come from and we were not further annoyed by the enemy that day. General Fitz Lee came up shortly after the enemy had been repulsed and formed a line of defense so as to protect our wagon trains and we occupied it all night.[9]

A Quiet Day

Early on the morning of the 8th Fitz Lee moved his division to the front and left me with mine as rear guard, and as soon as the wagons, artillery, and infantry had passed and the road was clear, I followed them, but as there was no cavalry in pursuit, I was not pressed or annoyed by the enemy at all, all day. Several times during the day I reported to Fitz Lee, then acting chief of cavalry, that the cavalry had all left the rear. I also asked to be allowed to take my division of cavalry and go to the rear and attack General Grant's supply trains. My scouts had reported that these trains were poorly guarded, and I believed then, as I believe now, that I should have been sent back upon this mission, but for some reason or other I was not allowed to go.

APPOMATTOX
The Surrender of the Army of Northern Virginia
to Lynchburg

About 10 A.M. a flag of truce came to me from the enemy in my rear, addressed to General R. E. Lee. An answer was returned through my lines in about two hours and this circumstance filled my soul with dread suspicion that the grand old Army of Virginia was about to be surrendered to that foe over which we had triumphed on many a hard-fought field. On reflection, the possibility of such a thing seemed to be doubly denied by the calm, manly and heroic bearing of every man in our little army, and I felt that the only answer which such a proposition could receive would be that of the Old Guard: We can die, but we cannot surrender. If the army had been consulted this would have been its answer!

A Meeting with Gordon

A little before dark I was ordered to take my command to the front to reinforce the cavalry then fighting at Appomattox Court House, and as I passed our infantry I saw that it had for the first time, on the retreat from Petersburg, gone regularly into camp and was making itself comfortable. This fact confirmed my suspicions as to the intentions of General R. E. Lee, and when I met General John B. Gordon soon after I had passed the first camps and told him what I had seen he defiantly said that his corps, although but a handful, was not whipped nor ready to surrender. He also stated that he had been sent for by General R. E. Lee and was then on his way to see him. I urged him to insist that I be allowed to go back that night and attack Grant's wagons and to this proposition he gallantly said: "If general Lee will allow me I will burn my wagons and mount my men on the mules and I will go back this night and join you in burning Grant's wagons. The idea is a good one and I will urge it on General Lee."

I felt better after this meeting with Gordon. Gordon was always cheerful and hopeful and ready to fight, and after Stonewall Jackson was taken away, John B. Gordon was the most able general that General R. E. Lee had left. The country had been drained by our own hungry troops, and if Gordon and I could have destroyed Grant's supply trains that night he would have been compelled to halt or retreat, for there was not enough rations in the country to have fed his army for one day.

I reached Appomattox Court House late at night and found Generals Roberts and Gary with their brigades in position on the western edge of the village. I took position on their right, sending out scouts to watch the roads toward Lynchburg to ascertain what the enemy was doing. Then I went to the house of my old friend Major McLean and spent the night talking over our war experiences. It was upon McLean's farm that the first battle of Bull Run [Manassas] had been fought and now he was about to furnish the stage whereon the last scene of the drama was to be exhibited. About 2 o'clock on the morning of the 9th Generals Gordon and Fitz Lee arrived, and being directed to my quarters by a sentinel in front of McLean's house, they rapped on the door, and being admitted by Lieutenant Winston, of my staff, they came into the parlor where I sat.

News

I saw by the dim light of several tallow candles, which were burning in the room, that something terrible had happened and I at once demanded the news. "To-morrow morning, General R. E. Lee desired us to say to you, he will either surrender the Army of

Northern Virginia or disperse it." I rose at once and informed these gentlemen that General Lee would not surrender me in the morning! My scouts had informed me that the Lynchburg Road was clear and I began making arrangements to move before daylight when General Gordon assured me that if I would wait until daylight that he would go with me, and with this understanding I got everything ready and waited.

To Lynchburg

About daylight other troops marched into the village and I rode to General Gordon and had some conversation concerning the attack we were about to make. About sunrise Gordon moved his little line to the front and his men met the enemy with their accustomed dash and confidence, capturing some prisoners and driving the cavalry back upon the infantry, when he was repulsed, but his repulse was more of a recoil than a defeat. When Gordon moved forward I charged the cavalry in my front and drove it off, capturing a good many prisoners, and I pushed on until I occupied the Lynchburg Road; then I changed front with my rear towards Lynchburg and pushed forward and attacked the enemy in the flank as he faced Gordon. In a few minutes I saw with my field glasses that Gordon had fallen back on Appomattox and then I saw the white flags. Then firing ceased and troops from the opposite lines began to walk freely about and then I saw all was over, so far as General Lee and his army were concerned. I had, however, received no instructions, and as I was then situated I determined that I would receive none and marched my command on to Lynchburg, where I arrived on the evening of the 9th.[10]

THE DISPERSION
Last Efforts to Revive a Sinking Cause
Arrest and Release

The surrender of General Lee was not the surrender of the Confederate States. Our president was still free and we had General J. E. Johnston and several other able generals in the field and there was still hope. Therefore I dispersed my little cavalry force, stating that I would push on rapidly to see the president and if their services were required I would return and collect them. They all assured me they would rally under the old banner whenever called, and I knew they were sincere. Each color-bearer took to his home the old battle flags and in their homes those dear old treasured flags can be found today.

Instructions from Breckenridge

After dispatching my command I left Lynchburg early on the morning on the 10th of April, and taking my staff rode to Danville,

Va., where I expected to overtake the president. When I reached there (on the morning of the 11th) I found that the president had gone to join the army under General Johnston, but I found there the Secretary of War, General John C. Breckenridge. To him I relayed all that had happened at Appomattox and got his approval of the course I had pursued. Then he commissioned me to return to central Virginia and collect all the soldiers who had not be paroled, organize them, and report to the governor of the state (Governor Smith was not present), and act under his orders if I could not be communicated with by the president or the War Department.

Captured

Under these instructions I returned to Staunton, Va., and had collected about five hundred men when the intelligence of Johnston's surrender reached me, and then the capture of the president occurred. Governor Smith had not returned to the state and there was no one to report to and no one to feed us. I resolved to march across the trans-Mississippi and report to General Smith. While my little command was getting ready at Swope's Depot, I rode to Hanover Court House to take leave of my wife and my baby, and in a few moments after I entered the house Federal troops surrounded it and carried me to Richmond as a prisoner. Upon reaching Richmond I learned that I had been charged with violating my parole, the Federals claiming that I had been surrendered by General Lee, at Appomattox; but by denying this and appealing to General Lee, who was in the city, I was released from this charge. General Lee having escaped from the forces surrendered my cavalry, which had escaped. General Lee then advised me to go to the valley and disperse my troops, and I made arrangements to give them parole certificates giving them parole, guaranteeing them immunity from arrest. I took an escort and proceeded to Staunton, and had Colonel Ball and the "rear guard" of the Army of Northern Virginia paroled, so that they might be "permitted to return to their homes unmolested."

Since the War

It is now more than eighteen years since these scenes have passed from the stage, where for four years they had engrossed the attention of the civilized world. Our blood had time to cool, and in a common interest, friends and foes are bound by ties of patriotism to one common country. Many changes have occurred to bring this about. The organizations of the two armies once so bitterly opposed to each other are now lost in the mingling and mixing of business and a common citizenship, and all the bitterness of the past which extended between the soldiers of the opposing armies is buried in the grave of the "Lost Cause," and forgotten.

Beware a Quarrel, But Being in...

There are many true and loyal Southern men who deeply deplored the hasty withdrawl of the Southern states from the Union, and who believed that the attack on Fort Sumter before the policy of President Lincoln was declared was ill-advised. Although a boy then I am not ashamed to confess that I was one of that number, but when the "die was cast," there was no choice left for us. We had to take the side of our own people. Although the president was elected by a sectional party I always had great faith in his patriotism, wisdom, and justice, and I believe that if the Southern people had not acted so hastily there would not have been found in the policy of the President Lincoln, an excuse for a withdrawal of a single state from the Union, and consequently there would have been no war.

The freeing of the slaves of the South by President Lincoln was undoubtedly an unauthorized and an illegal act, yet as an accomplished fact I regard it a great blessing to the South, and I believe that their old masters have been greatly benefited by the change. Thrusting suffrage upon these ignorant Negroes so soon after emancipation was a piece of contemptible spite on the part of that class of politicians who had not shared the dangers or glories of the battlefield with the manhood of the land, and this act they contributed as their blow against the vanquished armies of the Confederate States. The soldiers of the two armies have long since become reconciled to each other, and if politicians had not interposed General Grant and General Lee would have soon restored the Union and saved the country the expense and shame of the Freedman's Bureau and the carpetbagging robberies of reconstruction.

Major John Locher Knott
A veteran fighter of the Twelfth Virginia Cavalry Regiment, Knott was killed in the desperate fighting at High Bridge, near Farmville, Virginia, prior to the Confederate surrender at Appomattox Court House.

Courtesy of *A History of the Laurel Brigade*

Brigadier General James Dearing
The intrepid Dearing was killed in action on June 6, 1865, near Watson's farm on the road to Appomattox.

Courtesy of *A History of the Laurel Brigade*

Major Holmes Conrad
The youthful Conrad was promoted by Confederate President Jefferson Davis, on Rosser's recommendation, from private to major for his brilliant and death-defying actions near Ashland, Virginia, in 1864.

Courtesy of *A History of the Laurel Brigade*

General Thomas T. Munford
A graduate of Virginia Military Institute, Munford was continually overlooked for promotion in favor of Rosser. At one point Rosser had him court-martialed for alleged misconduct but he was cleared of all charges.

Courtesy of *A History of the Laurel Brigade*

Colonel E. V. White
Col. Elijah V. White, commander of the Thirty-fifth Virginia Cavalry (White's Battlion). A fierce fighter, he often charged into enemy units many times his number. He was wounded several times.

Courtesy of *A History of the Laurel Brigade*

Lieutenant Colonel Thomas Marshall
Thomas Marshall, one of Rosser's most trusted and bravest officers, was killed in the lower Shenandoah Valley, in 1864, less than six months before the end of the war.

Courtesy of *A History of the Laurel Brigade*

Major John W. Emmett
An assistant adjutant general on Rosser's staff, he was wounded several times during the war: at the Wilderness, in 1864, and again in the Shenandoah fighting Sheridan. The last wounding disabled him, for the remainder of the war.

Courtesy of *A History of the Laurel Brigade*

A postwar picture of General and Mrs. Thomas Rosser, dated May 28, 1880.

Courtesy of Mr. and Mrs. Douglas Cochran,
Hagerstown, Md.

Officers of the Laurel Brigade by Regiment

(The following lists were extracted from rosters prepared after the war by members of the individual company members.)

SEVENTH VIRGINIA CAVALRY

Company A

Ashby, Turner, captain, later brigadier general. Killed near Harrisonburg, Va., 6 June 1862.

Ashby, Richard, later captain, brother to Ashby. Mortally wounded at Kelly's Island in 1861, and died soon after.

Ashby, Luther, third lieutenant. Killed.

Fletcher, John, captain. Killed at Buckton, in 1862.

Hatcher, D. C., captain. Survived the war.

Turner, William F. Survived the war.

Company B

Winfield, John Q., first captain. Survived the war.

Magruder, J. H., second captain. Killed at Madison, Va.

Ligget, J. N., lieutenant. Survived the war.

Company C

Myers, Samuel B., captain. Wounded at Orange Court House, promoted major in 1863.

Myers, J. E., captain. Killed 7 May 1864.

Bowers, Phillip, first lieutenant. Survived the war.

Company E

Buck, Thomas H., captain. N/A

Simpson, Samuel, J., first lieutenant. N/A

Company F

Sheetz, George F., captain. N/A
Kuykendall, Isaac. Made captain at Battle of Cedar Mountain.
McDonald, Angus W., first lieutenant. Survived the war.

Company G

Mason, Dr. J. F., captain.
Davis, Sturgis, lieutenant, afterwards captain. From Baltimore
County, Maryland. Wounded.
Thrasher, Thaddeus, second lieutenant. Killed at Kernstown.

Company H

Sharp, I. C., captain. Killed 9 October 1864.
Sharp, Jacob, first lieutenant. Killed at Gettysburg.

Company I

Shans, E. H., captain. Accidentally killed in Rockingham County,
Va.
Roudabush, Noah D., first lieutenant. Died of typhoid fever in Hamp-
shire County, W. Va.
Lincoln, A. C., captain, after reorganization.

Company K

Miller, William, captain. Survived the war and died in Baltimore.
Koontz, H. R. T., second captain. Killed near Mt. Jackson, Va. (date
N/A).

ELEVENTH VIRGINIA CAVALRY

Company A

Turner, A. J. N/A
Seibert, J. B. N/A

Company B

Harness, William H., captain. Resigned. Capon Springs, W.Va.
Alex, S. H., first lieutenant. Survived the war.
Cartmell, M. B., promoted from first sergeant to captain. Killed 17
December 1863.

Company C

Pendleton, John R., captain. Survived the war.
Mitchell, E. S., first lieutenant. Survived the war.

Company D

McDonald, E. H., captain. Promoted to major and then lieutenant
colonel of regiment. Charles Town, W.Va.
Taylor, William, first lieutenant, promoted to captain. Ridgeville,
W.Va.

Company E

Hess, Joseph T., captain. N/A
Hooff, J. L., captain. N/A
McGuire, H. H., captain. Mortally wounded at Amelia Springs.
Brent, J. W., lieutenant. N/A
Hottel, G. W., lieutenant. Wounded and captured.
Hockman, William, lieutenant. Killed at Brandy Station.
Spiker, G. W. Killed at Spotsylvania.

Company F

McChesney, A. G., captain. Survived the war.
Ware, A. J., second captain. Survived the war.

Company G

Dangerfield, Foxhall A., captain. Wounded at Orange Court House, 2 August 1862; sabre cut on head and shot in left shoulder, captured, and exchanged. Wounded at Upperville, June 1863, at Baltimore and Ohio roundhouse; near New Creek, in 1864, and near Amelia Springs, 5 April 1865.
Mayse, Joseph, first lieutenant. Wounded at Jack's Shop on 1864, lost eye.

Company H

Pierce, A. M., captain. Survived the war.
Sherrard, Joseph, first lieutenant. Survived the war.

Company I

Ball, M. M., captain. Wounded.
Kirby, William H., lieutenant. Killed.
Moore, Alfred, lieutenant. Severely wounded.
Reid, Williams H. Survived the war.

Company K

Powell, William, lieutenant. N/A
Smith, Jack, second lieutenant. N/A

TWELFTH VIRGINIA CAVALRY

Harman, Asher W., colonel. Native of Staunton, Va. Wounded at Fleetwood Hill, near Brandy Station, 9 June 1863. A long-time prisoner of war.
Massie, Thomas E., lieutenant colonel. Native of Warren County, Va. Wounded several times, once severely.
Knott, John Locher, major. Native of Jefferson County, W.Va. Wounded and afterwards killed at High Bridge, near Farmville, Va.

Harman, Lewis, adjutant. Native of Staunton, Va. Commissioned later as captain of Company I. Later captured and held until the end of the war.

Company A

Isabel,———, captain. N/A
Henderson, John, captain. N/A

Company B

Baylor, R. W., captain. Badly wounded.
Rouss, Milton, first lieutenant. Wounded and captured at Brandy Station; spent some time in prison.

Company C

Ford, John H., captain. Wounded at Poolesville, Md., and at Jack's Shop.
Myers, W. H., first lieutenant. N/A

Company D

Kearney, H. W., captain. Wounded.
Engle, George, first lieutenant. N/A

Company E

Marshall, James, captain. N/A
McKay, J. C., first lieutenant.

Company F

Initially a mostly all-Maryland company. Its first captain was Harry Gilmore followed by James Clark. No other record is available.

Company G

Willis, A. M., captain. N/A
Swindler, A. C., first lieutenant, and later captain. N/A

Company H

Sipe, Emanuel, captain. Wounded at the Wilderness, May 1864; Valley, October 1864 held at Fort Delaware three months; made lieutenant colonel in 1864 and placed in command of Seventh Virginia Cavalry; captured in 1865 by Sheridan's army.
Randolph, E. C., first lieutenant. Wounded at Brandy Station, 1863, and at Cold Harbor.

Company I

O'Ferral, Charles T., captain. Transferred and promoted to a colonelcy; congressman from Virginia and governor of the state.
Eastham, Granville, first lieutenant. Desperately wounded at Brandy Station, died later.

THIRTY-FIFTH VIRGINIA CAVALRY

White, Elijah V., colonel commanding. Leesburg, Va. Wounded several times, but survived the war.

Ferneyhough, George N., major. Washington, D.C. Resigned 21 September 1864.

Myers, F. M., major. Succeeded Ferneyhough; formerly captain of Company C. Wounded 7 October 1864. Survived the war.

Company A

Myers, F. M., captain. Wounded at Mount Clifton, 7 October 1864. Survived the war.

Barret, William F., first lieutenant. Captured at Brandy Station, 9 June 1863. Prisoner for most of the war.

Company B

Chriswell, George W., captain. Montgomery County, Md. Wounded 9 June 1863, out for remainder of the the war.

Crown, J. R., first lieutenant. Frederick County, Va. Prisoner from 14 September 1863 to 11 June 1865. Survived the war.

Company C

Grubb, Richard B., captain. Formerly of Company A, 8th Virginia Infantry. Killed at Waterford, Va., 7 August 1863.

Dowdell, William F., second captain. Formerly orderly sergeant of Company A, Sixth Virginia Cavalry. Survived the war.

Grubb, Samuel E., first lieutenant. Formerly of Loudoun Cavalry, Sixth Virginia. Wounded and captured at Hillsboro, Va., January 1865. Survived the war.

Company D

Trayhern, James F., first captain. Resigned 25 November 1862.

Anderson, James, second captain. Prisoner of war 21 October 1862 to 30 December 1862 and again 9 June 1863 to 20 October 1864, then disabled for remainder of the war.

Company E

Grabill, John, captain. Wounded and prisoner from 9 June 1863 to 24 February 1865.

Strickler, H. M., first lieutenant. Methodist preacher from Baltimore Conference. Wounded 2 April 1865.

Company F

French, Marcellus, captain. Succeeded Captain Ferneyhough, who became major. Sick 10 September 1864 to 22 September 1864.

Watts, John W., first lieutenant. Killed at Brandy Station, 9 June 1864.

CHEW'S BATTERY

Chew, R. P., captain.
Thompson, James W., first lieutenant.

CHAPTER 1

1. Wade Hampton, a South Carolinian by birth, was wounded several times during the course of the war as commander of his cavalry brigade. He succeeded Jeb Stuart as commander of the cavalry corps after Stuart's untimely death on May 11, 1864. Fitz Lee, a nephew of Robert E. Lee, also commanded his own cavalry brigade, and near the end of the war became Gen. Lee's chief of the cavalry corps. Jubal Early is perhaps best known for his distinguished victory at Monocacy, Md., in 1864, in a drive toward Washington D.C. The fight served to alert defenders of the capital and his designed raid was called off.

2. The highly revered Ashby raised a company of volunteer cavalry to patrol the Potomac River after the famous John Brown raid at Harpers Ferry in 1859. When his native Virginia seceded his men became the Seventh Virginia Cavalry Regiment and he swiftly rose from captain to colonel. The June 1861 murder of his brother by a Union patrol infused in him an air of retaliation leading to future acts of uncommon bravery. He died early in the conflict, falling victim to Federal bullets near Harrisonburg, Virginia, on June 6, 1862.

3. A casual remark by Rosser when in command of the Fifth Virginia almost led to his death. After the fight at Catlett's Station in August, 22, 1862, in which the Fifth Virginia performed in a distinguished manner, a number of prisoners were rounded up. As the fighting wound down Rosser was asked "What shall we do with the prisoners?" To which he carelessly replied, "Kill 'em!" One of the prisoners overheard the remark and taking him at his word, told the others. A riot began as the Federals fought for their lives. One prisoner who still had a bayonet in his hand lunged at Rosser stabbing him in the arm and wounding his horse. The slip of the tongue was hastily explained and the prisoners settled down. See Capt. William N. A. McDonald, *A History of the Laurel Brigade* (Gaithersburg, Md.: Old Soldier Books, Inc., 1987), 198; Lea and Lynn de Grummond, *Jeb Stuart* (Pelican Publishing Co., 1979), 73. Just two days before the Seven Days' campaign opened Rosser was promoted to colonel and placed in charge of the Fifth Virginia Cavalry. Earlier, at Lewinsville, in September 1861, he earned a great amount of praise when he shot down one of Gen. George B. McClellan's observation balloons. See Douglas Southall Freeman, *Lee's Lieutenants*, 3 vols. (New York: Charles Scribner's Sons, 1942), 1:648; 2:209fn; hereafter cited as Freeman, *LL*. Rosser was generally a stranger to the Laurel Brigade. His reputation being received mostly through reports

that characterized him as an adventurous and successful warrior. He immediately appealed to the brigade through his demeanor, personal appearance, education, and his dash. His bearing exuded self-confidence. Rosser was always well mounted, and while he would never replace the brigade's old commander, Turner Ashby, the men knew they would be in capable hands. See McDonald, *A History of the Laurel Brigade*, 196–97; Frank M. Myers, *The Comanches* (Baltimore, Md.: Kelly, Piet and Co., 1871), 234.

For unknown reasons, Rosser omits his activities during Robert E. Lee's first and second invasions of the North. Actions at South Mountain, Antietam, and Gettysburg are lacking.

In December of 1862, a number of non-decisive raids were made by the cavalry near Fredericksburg, resulting in Stuart giving up on his plan and starting back to his base on the Rappahannock. Information came to him that the enemy had put a small force on the north side of the river to observe his action. Jeb decided to give them a first-person look. If it proved successful he would press on and continue northern raids. Fitz Lee was sent southward but had moved only a short distance when Stuart's scouts informed him that two Federal regiments were following the Confederate march, although at a safe distance. Fitz was turned around and sent at the columns with Hampton and Rooney Lee's troopers not far behind. Butler was sent toward Bacon Race Church to flank the enemy. Immediately as Butler left two Federal regiments appeared in Stuart's front. Deciding that his men could ride over them, he ordered Fitz Lee, with the First Virginia in the lead, to charge, clear the wooded area, and pursue. The First smashed into the enemy, killing some and capturing about 100. The Yanks turned and ran, and with their much fresher horses outran the Virginians, reaching Selectman's Ford, west of Manassas Station, and splashed through its chilly waters. The question now was, should the pursuit continue through the narrow, rocky and tricky passage? There was no hesitation on Rosser's part. With the Fifth Virginia in front, and with the charge sounded loud and clear by the bugler, his men smashed across the waters, received a weak spray of fire with no injuries, and reached the opposite banks. Then Fitz Lee came in immediate support and even Pelham, to the total consternation of all, drove his guns across the heretofore "uncrossable" ford. See Freeman, *LL*, vol. 2:405–06.

4. Kilpatrick was generally known to his subordinates as "Kilcavalry" for the reckless way he used his men in combat. See Patricia L. Faust, *Historical Times Encyclopedia of the Civil War* (New York: Harper and Rowe, 1986), p. 417.

5. The Kilpatrick raid on Richmond was made in late February and early March, 1864. He plotted to penetrate the Southern capital's weakened defenses and release thousands of Federal prisoners. The raid failed when the city's thin line of defense stiffened and the weather turned icy cold. See E. B. and Barbara Long, *The Civil War Day by Day* (New York: Da Capo Press, 1971), 469–72.

Private John Casler recorded that in the Brandy Station campaign, his uncle, R. D. Heironimus, of Rosser's Brigade, was severely wounded by being cut through the scalp with a sabre, laying the skull bare, but he recovered. See John O. Casler, *Four Years in the Stonewall Brigade*, edited by James I. Robertson, Jr. (Dayton, Ohio: Press of Morningside Bookshop, 1982), 165.

CHAPTER 2

1. The report of this capture of the wagon trains belonging to the Federal I and V Corps, reached Stuart on Sunday, Nov. 29, near Mine Run. Rosser destroyed 35 to 40 wagons, captured eight, along with ambulances, 230 animals, and

95 prisoners. See Theodore S. Garnett, *Riding with Stuart* (Shippensburg, Pa.: White Mane Publishing Co., 1994), 19; Freeman, *LL*, 3:274; A. A. Humphreys, *Gettysburg to the Rapidan, The Army of the Potomac, July 1863 to April 1864* (New York: Charles Scribner's Sons, 1883), 67. General R. E. Lee received a significant dispatch from Rosser at this time noting the capture of 280 mules, 150 prisoners and of great importance to the commander of the Army of Northern Virginia, that these wagons were observed heading for Orange Court House and not Chancellorsville, as Lee suspected. See Douglas Southall Freeman, *R. E. Lee*, 4 vols. (New York: Charles Scribner's Sons, 1935), 3:198, hereafter cited as Freeman, *REL*.

2. This is referred to as the Mine Run campaign in which Meade tried in vain to find a soft spot in Lee's defensive lines. Skirmishes occurred at Parker's store and New Hope Church before Meade gave up and retired across the Rapidan to go into winter quarters, in the full knowledge that his planned attack must now be given up. See Long, *The Civil War Day by Day*, 440–41.

3. Rosser inspired his men in the crossing of the small stream near Sangster's Station with a brilliant exhortation between the blinding flashes of lightning and deafening claps of thunder. As the rain beat down on them, Captain Hatcher's Co. A crossed the high waters and dashed up to the fort. Lt. Col. M. Beale, Eleventh Regiment, gave a loud cheer and using the flashes of lightning as a guide, along with flashes of enemy gunfire, crossed over and up the hill to capture the fort. Gallant Captain Cartmell, of Co. B, at the head of the first squadron was instantly killed, and several were wounded as the advance began. Following a brief celebration the wounded were attended to and Rosser pushed his jaded men and their mounts on toward Upperville. The rains continued to fall, but the thought of enemy pursuit pushed the column forward. See McDonald, *A History of the Laurel Brigade*, 211–13; Myers, *The Comanches*, 241–43.

4. Rosser's brigade led the advance down the South Branch on January 2, 1864, with the Eleventh Virginia in front, and the Seventh following. The road at the top of the mountain was blocked by fallen trees that had to be cleared by using axes. As this was being done scouts reported the wagon train moving toward New Creek on the same road Rosser occupied and which forked with the road to Petersburg and New Creek. Rosser rushed his forward-most regiments to the top of the gap. They observed the carelessly guarded train moving slowly along with teams of six mules pulling each of its forty wagons loaded with stores and ammunition. The Eleventh Virginia, followed by the Seventh, emerged from the cover of heavy woods and fell upon the train. Once alerted it lurched forward. Faster wagons tried to pass the slower ones, creating mass confusion along the road. Some upset, many collided, and mules became entangled and kicked furiously at everything. The mounted guard raced into the woods, but about seventy-five infantrymen jumped out of the wagons and began firing at the Virginians. However, a charge by the Eleventh soon quieted them and most surrendered. Rosser moved with Fitz Lee to Patterson's Creek, gathering cattle and more stores along the way and destroyed an abandoned enemy blockhouse. Lee intended to attack New Creek again but a severe winter snowstorm negated those plans. He returned to the Valley by way of Romney and Brock's Gap to Harrisonburg, accompanied by 400 head of cattle and 110 prisoners. A short rest was well received by the men after which Fitz Lee rejoined the Army of Northern Virginia. Rosser's brigade remained with Early. See McDonald, *A History of the Laurel Brigade*, 215–19; Myers, *The Comanches*, 248–50. During this winter there developed a minor contention between Rosser and Gen. Early involving wives. Rosser, deeply in love with his wife, invited her to camp during the winter to the general's antipathy. And while other officer's wives, such as Mrs. A. P. Hill and Mrs. John B. Gordon made frequent

visits, it disturbed Early to the point that he referred to it in a letter to Gen. Lee. New military action in January 1864, into western Virginia, served to dilute the problem. See Freeman, *LL*, 3:328.

5. Once again Rosser found himself crossing a mountain on the Moorefield to Alleghany Turnpike. McDonald records that nearing the top of the mountain the road was found to be blocked by fallen trees and guarded by a regiment of enemy soldiers. The Twelfth Virginia staged a frenzied attack and eventually forced its way through, sending the enemy reeling backwards on the road to Medley and toward the oncoming train. When alerted to Rosser's presence the Federals circled the wagons at Medley and with about 800 infantry and a few cavalry, set up a defense. Rosser, with 400 men, did not hesitate. He attacked with the Twelfth smashing the Federal rear. The first assault was turned back with some loss. However, the artillery arrived and as it dropped its shells among the train it created panic among its guards. Rosser's men leaped to the occasion. His dismounted warriors assaulted the fortification from all sides. The Federals threw down their arms and fled, leaving all of the wagons and forty-two prisoners. In the brief fight Rosser lost twenty-five men killed and wounded. The enemy dead and wounded that remained on the field were not recorded. See McDonald, *A History of the Laurel Brigade*, 219–21.

6. Leaving Petersburg, Rosser reached the Baltimore and Ohio Railroad line at the mouth of Patterson's Creek. Here he captured one guard and destroyed the bridges over the creek, the Potomac and the C and O Canal. By taking side roads to Moorefield he avoided Averill's main force that seemed to be avoiding him and at the same time giving the impression that it was in pursuit. Captain John McNeill arrived with his men and 300 head of cattle from beyond the Alleghany Mountains. See McDonald, *A History of the Laurel Brigade*, 220–21; Myers, *The Comanches*, 244–46.

7. Jeb Stuart was greatly pleased with the performance of Rosser's men and gave the following endorsement to his report: "The bold and successful enterprise herein reported furnishes additional proof of General Rosser's merit as a commander and adds fresh laurels to that veteran brigade, so signalized for valor already." See McDonald, *A History of the Laurel Brigade*, 220–21.

8. Rosser's writings do not touch on an incident that began on February 29, when he led his men across the Blue Ridge Mountains. This was the occasion of the famous Dahlgren-Kilpatrick raid on Richmond to free federal prisoners. Rosser pointed his column in that direction for pursuit under increasingly bad weather conditions. Most of his troopers, not dreaming of a long march, left camp without their coats. After dark the clouds thickened and a freezing rain began. Each man was turned into a living ice sculpture that made the column ghost-like in appearance as it moved along the country roads. The sleet continued to fall after midnight and let up at dawn as the men rode into Charlottesville for a short rest. Then it was on toward Richmond where camp was made six miles from the Confederate capital. Rosser gave pursuit for two weeks without luck then stopped at Gordonsville for a two-day rest. The brigade returned to the lush Shenandoah Valley on March 16, making camp at Lexington, where food was scarce but the water and air were excellent. See McDonald, *A History of the Laurel Brigade*, 220–21.

9. On May 4, 1864, Grant crossed the Rapidan bringing on the Battle of the Wilderness. The following day Rosser made camp on Lee's right at Mine Run and early that day had his men in the saddle moving toward Todd's Tavern, west of the Po River, and near the enemy. Before reaching the tavern a strong force of the enemy was encountered and a fight began between dismounted men on both sides of the road, and in a heavily wooded area. Despite Federal

artillery fire, Rosser's brigade pushed forward by fours, with the Twelfth Regiment in the lead, unaware that a complete Federal division was to his front. Col. Massey charged his men over a barricade where it fought in bloody hand-to-hand combat with pistols and sabers. The Federals fell back and as Rosser's men continued to push forward, they selected defensive positions that were shielded by artillery. When the enemy's retreat stopped and a desperate stand was made, the Seventh and Eleventh Regiments were committed to battle and the weight of their charge collapsed the Federal line. Men broke and ran. Many were captured in a pursuit that lasted for several miles. The chase went as far as Todd's Tavern where Rosser called it off and turned back to replenish his ammunition. Then the enemy began to harass Rosser's rear as he crossed the Po. It was from this fight that Rosser dubbed his men the "Laurel Brigade." Although, some survivors after the war insisted that the name was given to them earlier in the war in the Shenandoah Valley. See McDonald, *A History of the Laurel Brigade*, 223–24; Myers, *The Comanches*, 340; Garnett, *Riding with Stuart*, 52–53; *Battles and Leaders of the Civil War* (Secaucus, N.J.: Book Sales, Inc., 1985), vol. 4, 241.

10. Federal reports of Rosser's actions at Todd's Tavern credit his small command of three regiments, one battalion and one battery of artillery with repulsing one whole division that greatly outnumbered him. Later, two Federal divisions ganged up on Rosser and pushed him back beyond the Po River. General Lee acknowledged Rosser's efforts in his report saying, "a large force of cavalry and artillery on our right flank was driven back by Rosser's brigade." Casualties in this campaign included, according to McDonald, 114 killed, wounded and missing. Federal reports listed three officers and ninety-four men killed, twenty-seven officers and 389 men wounded and 187 missing. See McDonald, *A History of the Laurel Brigade*, 223–33; Myers, *The Comanches*, 277–79; Clifford Dowdy, *Lee's Last Campaign* (New York: Bonanza Books, 1960), 104–05.

11. Early on the sixth, Lee's troops were engaged hotly with Grant. On Rosser's orders, White's battalion galloped past the Chancellor plantation and entered the border of the Wilderness, a tangled mess of trees and shrub, woven so tightly that is was virtually impossible to pass through. White was to run over everything in his path. At one point White sent him a note asking, "How far do I go?" The reply was, "as far as [you] can." The brigade dashed forward sending the enemy pickets reeling backward and at one point a great distance from his support. Suddenly they came upon dismounted enemy cavalry sending volleys of fire into his ranks and inflicting some loss. Quick action by Rosser in sending in the Eleventh Regiment saved White. The Eleventh turned the enemy column back but abruptly came face-to-face with Grant's entrenched infantry. Its massive firepower riddled the Confederate ranks forcing it to retire. The Twelfth and the Seventh now combined to charge the soldiers and passed over the bodies of their fallen comrades. The struggle continued until Rosser ordered a battery to the field to fire over the heads of his men at the enemy. The Federals answered with six pieces of artillery, unleashing a terrible fire that tore up the ground on which Rosser's men fought frantically for their lives. Retreating to a wooded area he brought up 150 dismounted men under Major E. H. McDonald. As the formation was organized the Federal artillery shells rode over their heads and fell among the men forming in the woods, killing and wounding many of them. Confusion reigned as men screamed and scattered for their lives, defeating the plan. Rosser fully expected the enemy to mount a devastating charge, but it never materialized. Seated on his horse, next to the battery, Rosser assumed his men had punished the enemy

severely, putting a damper on further attacks. See McDonald, *A History of the Laurel Brigade*, 235–37.

CHAPTER 3

1. During the day of May 7, 1864, only a smattering of fighting occurred. However, that evening, Grant began his movement to sidestep Lee and move southward towards Spotsylvania Court House and in a few hours Lee moved out to meet him. On May 8, the Laurel Brigade joined Gen. Wade Hampton at Shady Grove and from then to September first became an integral part of Hampton's division, made up of Young's and Rosser's brigades. On May 8, Hampton's Brigade faced the full strength of the enemy, undaunted. Gen. R. E. Lee's order directed Early to attack the Federal left at Todd's Tavern. Hampton cooperated by sending Rosser to strike its right and rear while Young's Brigade hit the front. Both movements were carried off in grand fashion, pushing the enemy back, giving up its handsome camp and all of its rations. This fight marked the first engagement of the "Laurel Brigade," under Hampton, acting in concert with Early's successful attack at Todd's Tavern. Gen. Hampton was a great fighter and believed strongly in cavalry being used as mounted infantry, the horses being used to move the men from point to point as fast as possible, and the fighting being done on foot. He reasoned correctly that the development of the long-range rifle rendered the once glorious cavalry charge antiquated. Hampton's pickets were driven in on May 9 and after a vicious fight, the Yankees took control of the main road connecting Shady Grove with Spotsylvania Court House along with the bridge over the Po River. They were dislodged the following day, the tenth. Two days later the great and bloody battle of Spotsylvania Court House began. Hampton's men occupied Lee's left with sharpshooters and artillery posted to annoy the enemy as much as possible. On May 15 Rosser struck along the road leading to the Poor House and beyond to Fredericksburg. The Eleventh Regiment was in the lead and sustained several casualties including the regiment's adjutant Lt. Oliver M. Funston. See McDonald, *A History of the Laurel Brigade*, 238–39; Freeman, *LL*, 3:383–84.

   Myers writes that on Sunday, May 8, the whole brigade mounted early and skirmished near Todd's Tavern, but the enemy seemed to be shifting and refused to make a stand until about 10 A.M. when it was found to be in great numbers in a heavy stand of timber. Here, all the men with long-range guns were dismounted and ordered into the woods. Commanding the sharpshooters was Lieuts. Thomas W. White, of Co. C, [35th Virginia Cavalry]. Pretty soon the firing showed that a sharp fight was going on in the Wilderness. In a few minutes the mounted men were ordered forward to charge, but the enemy retired beyond the head waters and swamp of the Ny River. As the battalion moved forward they met some of the sharpshooters bearing to the rear all that was left of their accomplished leader, Lieut. White. He had been arranging his men in formation when shot by a rifleman hidden in the woods. Captain [Richard B.] Grubb assumed command of the company. Lieut. White and Rosser were not on good terms according to Myers. The reason being that Rosser excused from duty as militia some enlisted men until the company was organized and in actual service. White made no secret of his feeling to the colonel. This barrier between the two remained until the Battle of Brandy Station when White fought with brilliance and audacity, thus gaining completely Rosser's confidence and goodwill.

2. Hancock advanced at 4:35 A.M. at quick time with arms at right shoulder shift with bayonets fixed, the Sixty-sixth New York comprised the advanced skirmishers. The mass of Federal soldiers covered the ground in front of the Confederates. On the Federal right the Twenty-first Virginia Infantry, on high ground, fired at the Second Delaware and killed Lt. Col. David Stickler. When

support arrived and the line advanced, the Virginians had gone. Eventually, the thin Rebel ranks yielded to superior numbers and shuttered at the ear-splitting screams of the advancing enemy as it tore away at the salient line, and in one sector most of the Stonewall Brigade was captured, along with about 4,000 of their comrades. Fighting raged past midnight in the "Bloody Angle of Spotsylvania." In all, twenty-four Federal brigades attacked the small salient. On this day, Federal losses numbered 6,800 killed, wounded and missing; the Confederates 5,000. See William D. Matter, *If It Takes All Summer* (Chapel Hill, N.C., and London: The University of North Carolina Press, 1988), 200–06; Long, *The Civil War Day by Day*, 499–500. The general assaults on the Confederate lines began in earnest on May 10 and raged with alien fury. The "Mule Shoe," in the center of the Rebel line was pounded relentlessly, being breached once but the bluecoats were thrown back. On the following day a cold rain fell as the men caught their breath. At dawn of the twelfth Grant turned loose a full assault on Lee's line in a fight in which thousands of muskets were fired rapidly at close range. Bullets shattered a grove of trees behind the Confederates, wooden breastworks shattered into a thousand pieces and dead men's bodies were so pulverized by shot and shell that they disintegrated. On May 16, Sheridan worked his way around Lee's right with a large number of cavalry and struck Stuart at Yellow Tavern, a short distance north of Richmond. Stuart was killed in this furious action. When word was received of Stuart's death, a great despondency spread over the brigade. However, there was no time for pause as Grant continued his movement south. Hampton's division was now commanded by General Butler, of South Carolina, and Gen. Hampton was placed in command of the cavalry corps. There was sporadic fighting over the next week. The "Laurel Brigade" protected Lee's left wing at this time. See McDonald, *A History of the Laurel Brigade*, 239; Long, *The Civil War Day by Day*, 498. When Rosser and his men arrived on the fourteenth they entered the Federal Fifth Corps Hospital area and removed about eighty Confederate wounded who were able to walk. The medical attendants who were not displaying a medical badge on their uniforms were captured. Rosser then allegedly received an oral promise from the commanding Federal medical officer that the wounded Yankees would be considered prisoners until later exchanged. After the war Hampton complained that this promise was not carried out, perhaps, because Rosser's men made off with most of the rations that had been left for the wounded. The doctor in charge of the Second Corps sent word to Hancock of Rosser's presence, and the 12th New Jersey was dispatched to the hospital area on a dead gallop. Rosser, asking a Federal medical nurse directions to the road to Fredericksburg, withdrew. It was nearly dark when the New Jersey troops arrived and in the dim light, surgeon Thomas Jones of the 18th Pennsylvania Reserves, was mistaken for a Rebel and was shot and killed. The infantrymen shared their rations with their wounded comrades. See Matter, *If It Takes All Summer*, 287–88.

3. Following an encounter at Wright's Tavern on May 21, Hampton attempted to stay in front of Grant. At the bridge near Hanover Junction the men fought bravely against heavy odds until relieved by Lee's infantry. Hampton then moved to Lee's left. Heavy rains fell on the twenty-fifth and twenty-sixth making roads unpassable. At 11 P.M. on the twenty-seventh the brigade was again on the move toward Anderson's Ford, riding through Ashland and going into camp at Atlee's Station, within six miles of the Confederate capital. Hampton, now in command of all of Lee's cavalry, was ordered to ascertain if enemy infantry has crossed the Pamunkey River. He sent "Rooney" Lee's division along with the brigades of Rosser, Butler, and Wickham toward the enemy.

Two miles from Haw's Shop they ran into enemy pickets that were easily driven back on the main body. Rosser and Wickham's men, fighting on foot, backed up by artillery worked the ground, and both sides suffered light losses. However, it wasn't long until the Federals, in heavy numbers, reclaimed the ground they had just lost. Rosser's veterans withdrew in good order, but most of Butler's men, being raw recruits, were attacked by the flank, fell into great disorder and suffered for it. Hampton went in and brought them out, Butler, being still absent due to injury. Rosser lost eight killed and about twenty wounded. See McDonald, *A History of the Laurel Brigade*, 242–43.

In Myers' writings he paints the following picture of Haw's Shop. As the corps went into position Chew's battery took position in an open field about 200 yards in front of a heavy pine forest. Gen. Hampton rode along the line, saluted and said to Col. White, "Good morning, Colonel, we've got the Yanks where we want them now!" However, Myers said in only 15 minutes the boot was quickly on the other foot. The storm of shot and shell that howled madly over and around them was terrific and very soon two splendid men, Lieut. Strickler, of Co. E, and Jack Howard, of Co. A, [35th Virginia], were wounded. Strickler in the knee and Howard in the face with the big end of an exploded shell that came bounding along the field. Several horses were killed. As to Gen. Butler's new recruits from South Carolina, Myers records that in their first time under fire their horses stampeded, and their queer bundles of clothing scattered through the pines in every direction as they stood their ground, fighting off the first wave of Federal cavalry. Only when the 6th Corps of Yankee infantry came against them did they withdraw on Hampton's orders. The cavalry corps, Myers said, was beginning to learn the ways of its new commander. Stuart usually did his work with whatever force he had at hand. Hampton preferred sending every available man to the point of operations. Under Stuart stampedes were frequent. Under Hampton they were unknown leading to great admiration for the new leader. See Myers, *The Comanches*, 290–91.

In Custer's report of this fight, dated July 4, 1864, he tells of meeting the Confederates in force at Haw's Shop and a fight against superior odds in a wooded area. Eventually he got the upper hand and drove the enemy in great disorder. He camped the night of the twenty-seventh of May on Crump's Creek, when General Gregg's Second Division was attached by Rebel cavalry, in force. Custer then went to his assistance, but found the thick underbrush and woods prevented a successful maneuver. Dismounting his entire brigade Custer formed lines, crossed the Richmond Road at right angles with the First and Sixth Michigan on the right and the Fifth and Seventh on the left. Gregg's tired troopers, opened a line for Custer's men to occupy as the fighting reached a fever pitch. Then Custer ordered an advance in the face of heavy Confederate fire that quickly stalled. Custer again ordered an advance and this time his troopers poured across the rough ground and dislodged the enemy, that he says withdrew leaving many of its dead and wounded on the field. A pursuit was then ordered until the Confederates were out of the range of Federal guns. Custer said his examination of the ground ascertained enemy losses far greater than any other previous engagement. Custer's loss was sizable, and also more than any other similar engagement. This included the wounding of several of his fine company commanders. See *War of the Rebellion: A Compilation of the Official Records of the Union and Confederate Armies*, ser. 1, vol. 36, pt. 1, 821–22; hereafter cited as *OR*.

4. McDonald records that Confederate losses from the first of May numbered about 300 killed, wounded and captured, and an even greater number of horses had been killed or disabled. Yet, he says, the ranks continued to swell.

Army rations were poor and in short supply, and forage for their animals was also scarce. After a hard day's fight, many hours would be spent searching for food for the men and horses. See McDonald, *A History of the Laurel Brigade*, 244–45.

Conrad's promotion brought him to be inspector general of the Laurel Brigade. When the war began he enlisted in the Co. A, of the First Virginia Cavalry, from Frederick County, Va. He became adjutant of the Seventh Battalion in August of 1862. The 7th eventually evolved into the 11th Virginia Regiment of the Laurel Brigade. See McDonald, *A History of the Laurel Brigade*, 247fn. McDonald recounts that Conrad seized the 11th's flag and shouted, "Men, save your colors!" With the banner waving he rode directly into the enemy's advance column, penetrating the first file. The Federals failed to fire at him, perhaps due to his audacity, the clouds of dust and outright admiration for his bravery. They may have been distracted by the rushing onset of his fellow graycoats who were right behind him. The "Bath Squadron" under Captain Foxhall A. Dangerfield, of the 11th, inspired by Conrad's conspicuous bravery, slammed into the Yanks and dispersed them in all directions. See McDonald, *A History of the Laurel Brigade*, 247–48; Myers, *The Comanches*, 245–48.

5. The Federals began the burning of the Shenandoah Valley at this time, and Stanton had been captured and Gen. W. E. "Grumble" Jones, a former commander of the brigade had been killed. On June 7, Gen. Sheridan moved with two divisions to join with General Hunter to break up a valuable Confederate supply line, the Virginia Central Railroad and also the James River Canal. Hampton's men knew the Yankees were taking aim at capturing and destroying Charlottesville and Gordonsville, with their rail lines, then smash Lynchburg. On the ninth, Hampton along with Fitz Lee and several batteries of horse artillery were sent to assault the plunderers. See McDonald, *A History of the Laurel Brigade*, 250; Myers, *The Comanches*, 308.

CHAPTER 4

1. Hampton's plan was to cover Lee's left and his right flank and to drive the enemy back once he attempted a move on to Gordonsville. He would move to his left, concealing his real intent at attacking him at Clayton's store once the two divisions were together. See McDonald, *A History of the Laurel Brigade*, 251, 308–10; *Battles and Leaders*, 4:237–39. McDonald records that when dawn broke Hampton was ready with Butler and Young's brigades and soon a message form Fitz Lee indicated that he was moving to attack Custer's Seventh Michigan Cavalry. He adds, "According to Hampton's report the Confederates repulsed the Federals, but Sheridan reported a different story. Up to 9 P.M. the fight went well for Hampton until Custer, with about 1,200 men, got in behind him, but the South Carolinians confronted Custer, pushing him back. Colonel R. Preston Chew's battery, positioned on a hill north of and in front of the station, opened fire, delaying Custer's exit by crippling his horses and stopping the wagons, and driving them back on the station. When Custer made a second try at escaping, Rosser appeared, wheeled to the left of the Federal column, the First Michigan, and drove it back on Fitz Lee who was coming up from the other side of the station. Here the Confederates recaptured many wagons and five caissons. The desperate charge of Fitz Lee's Sixth Virginia Cavalry, known as the Clarke Cavalry, is underscored by its loss of half of its men as it charged an enemy battery. A final assault was ordered by Rosser with White's men. Hampton rode up and denied it. That evening, assisted by some infantry, Custer attempted to dislodge Hampton from his new position west of the station and facing Sheridan who was moving up. After one of these unsuccessful assaults that was repulsed by Hampton, Rosser led his

brigade in a charge and at this point received his leg wound, putting an end to that movement. As the fighting waned, and Sheridan's infantry appeared on the field, Custer withdrew and made camp along the Pamunkey. See McDonald, *A History of the Laurel Brigade*, 252–54; Dowdy, *Lee's Last Campaign*, 307–09; *Battles and Leaders*, 4:233–36 and 237–39; *OR*, ser. 1, vol. 36, pt. 1, 823.

General Early, in his memoirs, echoes Rosser's assessment of the Trevilian fight, saying that "Hampton's defeat would have opened the door for Sheridan to Lynchburg and it would have fallen before he could have reached it in time to do any good." See Early, *Jubal Early's Memoirs*, 379fn. With Rosser's wounding, command of the brigade fell to Col. R. H. Dulaney, of the 7th Virginia. General Lee expressed his regrets to Rosser in a letter dated July 28, 1864. See McDonald, *A History of the Laurel Brigade*, 254; Myers, *The Comanches*, 301; Freeman, *LL*, 3:522 and fn. Myers' account of the Trevilian episode points out that "old Wade," as Hampton was often affectionately referred to, had never been whipped yet, and his men believed that Sheridan was not the man to do it, even though he had command of all the U.S. Cavalry. And, also that Sheridan was superior to the Confederates, not only in numbers, but arms and equipment. Sheridan's men carried repeating rifles and revolvers, while Hampton's men carried only the Sharpe's carbine and sabre. Many had only a common infantry musket. Rosser's Brigade was the only one in the division thoroughly equipped with revolvers and improved carbines, and they had been captured from the enemy. At this point in the war the Confederacy was too poor and unskilled in the manufacture of arms to keep pace with the wealthy North. At one point while the Federals were falling back White's men, rushing pell-mell forward, reached a hill about a mile from the station and observed a supposed Confederate battery on the right, in full play and unsupported with a large number of the enemy in a woods below him, and a strong force posted behind a brick kiln to the left. White gave orders for a plank fence on the right of the road to be pulled down. The battery was only two hundred yards away and White observed the force behind the brick kiln growing ever stronger. At this moment General Hampton thundered over the hill screaming, "Colonel White, what are you doing?" "Going to support that battery," said the colonel. "Get away from here colonel, that is a Yankee battery!" Immediately White proceeded to "get away." See Myers, *The Comanches*, 293–301.

2. McDonald records that Rosser was still in pain and suffering from his wounds when he returned to the field. On October 5, with 600 men in the saddle, he reinforced Early at Waynesboro, Va. See McDonald, *A History of the Laurel Brigade*, 320; Freeman, *LL*, 3:585. Hill's artillery signaled the beginning of combat at 5 P.M. Hampton advanced, facing several ranks of veteran infantry positioned behind strong earthworks. Hampton's dismounted troopers barreled ahead, answering the enemy's fire with blistering volleys of their own. In a short period of time the bluecoats were dislodged and retreating toward Ream's Station. As Hill advanced from the west side, Hampton wheeled his men about and brought them in behind the enemy. His forward movement was impeded somewhat by the broken ground, felled trees and brush, but he succeeded in driving the enemy from behind its fortifications. In one of those comic twists of fate that often occur in battle, Hampton's extreme right found itself alongside Hill's extreme left, where there were two Twelfth Virginia units: Hill's Twelfth Infantry, and Hampton's Twelfth Cavalry. Smiles and greeting were exchanged and then a friendly competition as to which would be allowed the honor of charging the enemy to their front. That was settled when Hill's big guns issued forth an ear-shattering blast over which the order to "charge" was given. Both Twelfths advanced, undaunted at the enemy's ferocious fire. At first the two advanced evenly. But, when the infantry stopped near the Federals to deliver its volley, the cavalry never stopped. With pistols cocked

and sabers in hand they assaulted the breastworks, and absorbed one volley after which the enemy ran away. See McDonald, *A History of the Laurel Brigade*, 273–74; Myers, *The Comanches*, 312–15.

3. This raid was referred to by the men as the "Newspaper Raid," made with the purpose of obtaining some Northern newspapers. McDonald says he does not believe a single paper was captured. See McDonald, *A History of the Laurel Brigade*, 284–85.

4. Rosser's cattle raid was determined "brilliant." It plated many a fine hot meal for the hungry Confederates. In all, 2,486 head were carried off. His opposition was furnished by about 400 men of the District of Columbia Cavalry, and the barricade indicated the Confederate approach was suspected and measures were prepared for opposition. The charge by the Eleventh Regiment into a torrent of fire was not without casualties. The Seventh counted three killed and fifteen wounded; the Twelfth more than that. The horse of Orderly Sergeant Seth Timberlake, Co. B, of the Twelfth, the "Fighting Sergeant," was shot dead and fell upon him. It required a half dozen of his comrades to remove the animal and free the rider. After passing the first line of defense the following incident occurred as Rosser approached the cattle herd. Riding at the head of the brigade, Rosser sent Private Cary Seldon, of Co. B, the Twelfth, forward with a white handkerchief hanging on the point of his sabre. In a loud voice he called to the Yankees, "General Rosser demands your surrender!" The officer in command yelled his reply in a loud, clear voice, "Go to hell!" That vocal blast was immediately followed by a blast from his guns. That signaled the Confederate charge, and a retreat by the Federals who rode among the cattle firing their guns and scattering the beeves. See McDonald, *A History of the Laurel Brigade*, 286–88. Also, at this time the veteran Federal Fifth Corps left the lower Valley by way of Front Royal. Sheridan remained strong, while Early had lost Anderson and Kershaw, who had been recalled to the Army of Northern Virginia. See Freeman, *LL*, 3:576, 590 and 593. The daring raid at the rear of the Federal army brought some comment from the officer corps. On September 17 Gen. B. F. Butler wrote to Gen. Grant: "Yesterday three brigades of Hampton's Cavalry turned our left and struck the cattle corral about seven miles below City Point and captured about 2,000 cattle and our telegraph construction party." The Federals gave pursuit and managed to tangle with a small rear guard along the Jerusalem Plank Road, but withdrew after a short skirmish. Only a few scattered cattle were found and returned. The Federal lower-level officers in "explaining away" this loss, credited Hampton with upwards of 14,000 men, mostly infantry! See McDonald, *A History of the Laurel Brigade*, 293–94; Myers, *The Comanches*, 374.

5. Late in August, Early skirmished with Sheridan's troopers at Charles Town, W.Va., and in the northern end of the Shenandoah Valley. On August 25, Early threatened another invasion of Maryland by posting forces near Williamsport, Md., and Shepherdstown, W.Va. There were skirmishes at Kearneysville, Shepherdstown and Halltown, W.Va. On Friday, August 26, Early found Sheridan in a strong position near the Potomac River, decided to move back toward Bunker Hill, W.Va., and Stephenson's Depot, Va. On August 29, Sheridan won an engagement at Smithfield Crossing, then shifted toward Berryville, threatening Winchester. Skirmishing took place at Martinsburg, W.Va., on August 31. As the threat to Winchester built, and a Federal thrust at the valley became obvious, Early was shaken by a request from Robert E. Lee for the return of troops loaned him for use at Petersburg. Lee also asked President Jefferson Davis for Negro substitutes. "Our ranks," he said, "were constantly being diminished by battle and disease." Early, as requested, released R. H. Anderson's Corps on September 3. Meanwhile,

Sheridan's forces were growing. Skirmishing broke out in and around Winchester, but by the twelfth neither side seemed to make progress. On learning of Early's loss, Sheridan, with Grant's approval, planned to cut Early's lines of communication and supply south of Winchester. On September 17, Early is outnumbered 2 to 1, moved toward Martinsburg. Sheridan then struck a separated Confederate force north of Winchester. After an all-day fight, Early withdrew with heavy casualties, as Sheridan snapped at his heels. On September 21 and 22, Early clashed again with Sheridan in and near Fisher's Hill, and at Front Royal. Finally, Sheridan drove Early backwards with heavy losses, toward New Market, where more skirmishing occurs in the vicinity over the next three days.

On the twenty-eighth, Rosser was ordered to report to Early. See Long, *The Civil War Day by Day*, 564–75. Throughout this period the odds at all times favored the Federals. Early, at best, never had more than 16,000 men. In sharp contrast, Sheridan controlled a war machine consisting of 35,000 infantry and artillery and about 8,000 cavalry, to which the Military District of Harpers Ferry added another 5,000. Odds favoring Sheridan of about 3 to 1. See Gary W. Gallagher, essays by Gary Gallagher, Jeffery D. Wert, A. Wilson Green, Robert K. Krick, and Dennis E. Frye, *Struggle for the Shenandoah* (Kent, . Ohio, and London, England: Kent State University Press, 1991), 24.

Rosser's Brigade arrived on Oct. 5 and was temporarily attached to Fitz Lee. Early found that Rosser's mounts were jaded and worn from hard service and he could field only about 600 men for service. See Early, *Jubal Early's Memoirs*, 435. Fitz Lee was seriously wounded at Winchester, giving the command of his division to Rosser, with Col. R. H. Dulaney commanding the Laurel Brigade. Rosser found the division thinned out from much fighting with Sheridan. See McDonald, *A History of the Laurel Brigade*, 300; Freeman, *LL*, 3:596. At this time Confederate commands were also beginning to thin out. With Fitz Lee out, Brig. Gen. William C. Wickham resigned to take a seat in the Confederate House of Representatives; Stuart was feuding with "Grumble" Jones, and Munford and Rosser were distant. At First Manassas, Rosser was a first lieutenant and Munford a lieutenant colonel. Rosser received future promotions while Munford did not. Now, they found that they must cooperate with each other for the good of the Southern cause. See Freeman, *LL*, 3:596.

6. At this time the Virginians were greatly angered by what they saw in the Shenandoah Valley. Sheridan's men were burning everything in sight—barns, homes, stackyards and grain. Huge clouds of smoke hovered over the valley like black birds of prey, marking the path of Sheridan's destroyers. See McDonald, *A History of the Laurel Brigade*, 300; Early, *Jubal Early's Memoirs*, 436. Rosser overtook Custer's men at about 3 p.m. at Mill Creek. Col. Dulaney, with part of the Seventh and White's Battalion, crossed a lower ford and advanced to the Federal rear and prepared to attack when a large number of Federal cavalry, coming to Custer's aid, arrived and blocked Dulaney's way. An instant charge, led by Capt. Dan Hatcher, of the Seventh, surprised the enemy, driving them back up the stream to a hill near the main body. Beyond was a field full of sheep and cattle, a prize the men would fight for. See McDonald, *A History of the Laurel Brigade*, 302; Myers, *The Comanches*, 336.

7. Major General Wesley Merritt said his movement north, on the eighth, was made without particular incident except by the enemy's cavalry, specifically that of Rosser. The Confederates made several bold charges at Custer's troopers and later on Merritt. On the ninth, Sheridan directed his chief of cavalry, Maj. Gen. Alfred Torbert, to attack and beat the enemy's cavalry or "get whipped himself." Torbert engaged Rosser and Lomax and eventually, with help, drove the Rebels over twenty miles. See *Battles and Leaders*, 4:513. In

this engagement, like so many others that he fought, Rosser was outnumbered. In this engagement he mounted no more than 1,500 to 1,700 troops; the Federals easily counted 4,000. Also, the enemy was on fresh mounts and armed with the Spencer seven-shot carbines that were effective at about 1,000 yards. See McDonald, *A History of the Laurel Brigade*, 305. Rosser aligned his force as follows, Wickham's Brigade, under Col. Munford held the left, with its right touching on the Back Road. On the right of this road were posted two pieces of Thompson's Battery, under Capt. J. W. Carter, with support by William Payne's small brigade of about 300 men. Rosser's right was held by the Laurel Brigade commanded by Col. R. H. Dulaney. The Seventh Virginia held the center of this brigade in support of dismounted sharpshooters from the Eleventh Regiment. On its right was placed the Twelfth Virginia, mounted in single line of battle with White's Battalion mounted on its left. Sheridan's orders to Gen. Torbert, commanding Merritt's and Custer's divisions of cavalry, were to "start out at daylight and whip the Rebel cavalry or get whipped himself." See McDonald, *A History of the Laurel Brigade*, 305. In camp that night on the high ground near Tom's Brook, Rosser's men reflected on the day's carnage and their present situation. The enemy was to their front in great numbers as could be determined by its thousands of campfires, and Gen. Early was 25 miles behind them. Rosser considered leaving the field that night and was encouraged to do so by some of his officers. However, he considered his orders from Early to imply otherwise. See Myers, *The Comanches*, 338.

8. In sneaking up on Custer, Rosser had entrusted one of his faithful scouts to meet him along the road near the Federal camp to report on just where the enemy was. However, the scout mistook Rosser's men for Federal cavalry in the darkness and remained hidden in a wooded area. Operating in a "blind," so-to-speak, Rosser divided his men into two groups for the assault that was to begin at his signal. As the attack began, some of Col. Oliver Funston's men mistook the first group for the enemy and opened fire. A bugler in Rosser's group became confused and seeing his people hesitant about charging forward, sounded a brisk charge, drowning out the frantic screams of officers to cease fire. Not until there were several wounded was the mistake corrected. See McDonald, *A History of the Laurel Brigade*, 309. As Federal sharpshooters advanced at first light, Lieutenant Nicholas Dorsey, of Co. B., White's Battalion, moved the brigade to a position in the middle of the road along Tom's Brook. Lieutenant [G. W., Co. B] Criswell, with forty men, held a line about one-quarter of a mile in length with only 40 men. He fell back as the Twelfth was driven in and as he was outflanked by a fast moving column of Federals. The battery of Captain James W. Thompson was overrun and captured as he fought bravely, giving Rosser's men a chance to retreat safely. See Myers, *The Comanches*, 338–40. General Early recorded a loss of nine pieces of artillery, although Sheridan boasted of eleven. See *Battles and Leaders*, 4:525.

9. By the seventeenth, Early's army had just about used up all of his provisions and was put in a position of either moving back to resupply, or attack. He chose the latter. See Freeman, *LL*, 3:597. Early's attack had John Gordon moving east under cover of darkness around the edge of the Massanutten, and across the Shenandoah River then north to the Cooly farmhouse. He was to deploy and take Belle Grove, about a mile south of Middletown, on the valley pike. His special mission was the capture of Sheridan, believed to be headquartered at Belle Grove. Kershaw was to march east through Strasburg, turn northeast across Cedar Creek at Bowman's Mill and attack to Gordon's left. Rosser, with his and Wickham's men, was to strike the Union cavalry opposite the Confederate left. Lomax was ordered via Front Royal to cooperate with the forces on the valley pike. See Freeman, *LL*, 3:598. When the action ceased and an eerie lull fell over the battlefield, many of Rosser's exhausted

men lay down by their horses and went to sleep. Contrary to Rosser's writings after the war, McDonald says the build-up of the enemy was not perceived by either Early or Rosser. It was 3 P.M. when the silence was shattered by Federal cannon aimed at Funston's men, as Sheridan surged back at Early. See McDonald, *A History of the Laurel Brigade*, 304. Early records that when the early morning fog lifted on the nineteenth it revealed the enemy's position to be exceptionally strong. Later when Federal guns began to open on his lines, he ordered all of his guns to concentrate on the enemy's guns. See Early, *Jubal Early's Memoirs*, 445.

In Myers' account he tells of the capture of great quantities of artillery, arms and camp equipage, many prisoners; so many, in fact, that it surprised Early that his army had routed Sheridan. Sheridan, on the other hand, was dumbfounded at his losses, all in one day. As it would eventually turn out, it was one of the most remarkable cases ever for a Yankee army to take a beating and be routed, and then return, on the same day, and thrash the foe. See Myers, *The Comanches*, 341–42. During the fight Rosser was galloping through the woods and brush when a very tall major in Federal garb suddenly appeared in front of him. The demand for the captured officer's sword was given instant attention. However, at that same instant a body of six or seven bluecoats came charging to the rescue of the major. Confident that they had saved the day for their officer they gave out with an ear-splitting scream of victory, but is was premature. Hidden by some nearby trees was a body of Rosser's cavalry that sprang a trap at the last minute, capturing the astonished Federals and squelching their "victory chorus." See McDonald, *A History of the Laurel Brigade*, 317–18. As Early's infantry ground to a halt at Fisher's Hill, Rosser's command retired in good order to the Back Road. Then the infantry was ordered back on the road to New Market, leaving Rosser at Fisher's Hill until mid-morning on the twentieth. When the enemy did not challenge him, he moved to a line along Stony Creek, across from Columbia Furnace. Early's losses at Cedar Creek were twenty-three pieces of artillery, numerous ordnance and medical wagons, 1,860 men in killed and wounded and about 1,000 prisoners. The Confederates took 1,500 prisoners. Early wrote after the war that the loss was partially due to demoralization caused by the plunder of the enemy's camps and because the men used bad judgement on when to retire. On the twenty-first he wrote the following report, "We had within our grasp a glorious victory, and lost it by the uncontrollable propensity of our men to plunder, in the first place, and the subsequent panic among those who kept their places...." Still, Early knew he had committed a grievous blunder. When he sent his report to Richmond he admonished his engineer Jed Hotchkiss, in the engineer's words... "not to tell General Lee that we ought to have advanced in the morning at Middletown, for, said he, we ought to have done so." See Freeman, *LL*, 3:608–09; Early, *Jubal Early's Memoirs*, 450–51. Losses to the Confederate officer corps were dreadful. Brig. Gen. James Conner, a brigade commander in Maj. Gen. J. B. Kershaw's Division, was wounded on the thirteenth in the same leg as during the Seven Days, and lost his leg. Brig. Gen. Cullen A. Battle, a brigade commander under Maj. Gen. Stephen D. Ramseur, was lost on the nineteenth when a bullet shattered his knee, and Ramseur was mortally wounded. Worst of all he could not be removed from the field and was left in the hands of the enemy. Friends in the Union army carried him to Sheridan's headquarters where surgeons worked without success to save his life. In his last moments he sent a message to his young wife and the baby he had yet to see. See Early, *Jubal Early's Memoirs*, 450–51; Freeman, *LL*, 3:609–10.

10. On the eleventh Rosser left the Eleventh Virginia at Cedar Creek and marched the rest of his command to New Town, below Winchester, where he encountered Federal cavalry and drove it back on a larger body of Federal infantry, conducting a brisk skirmish. The Eleventh was ordered to advance down the Back Road and ran into Custer again. Engaging the high bank of the south side of Cedar Creek the Eleventh held the Federals at bay until the Seventh and Twelfth arrived and helped drive Custer away. Assuming that the enemy was on the Middle Road, he left the Eleventh alone on the Back Road. Watching the large body of Federals now occupying the Middle Road, Rosser was unaware that Custer's whole division was racing up the Back Road directly at the Eleventh. The Eleventh, under Major E. H. McDonald, one-half mile from Rosser, felt the brunt of Custer's force, deployed across the valley floor in echelon, as it swept in on him. McDonald's men used the safety of trees and farmhouses and managed to hold their ground. Custer's main body now swept forward and met the second squadron who put up a spirited fight before being shoved backwards, but were rallied by Captain Dougherty. Custer's men remained resolute, pressing forward and breaking the first squadron. Captain Foxhall Dangerfield's first squadron, composed of two veteran companies, mostly mountain men, flew at the Federals in a furious assault that stopped the enemy, and sent it reeling back upon fresh units coming to its assistance. At once, Custer saw how small a force he faced, and sent in even more troopers and gradually the entire division advanced. The Eleventh fell back in disorder. Relief came as the rest of the Eleventh, along with the Seventh and Twelfth, rushed to McDonald's aid but by now Custer was beyond Rosser's left. The Confederate relief approached the battlefield in single file and was unable at first to make good progress. At this point the gallant Colonel Marshall, at the head of the widely scattered Seventh, dashed at Custer's men in a futile assault that was overrun by the bluecoats. Marshall was surrounded but in order to avoid capture he bolted away but was delivered a mortal wound. The Confederates withdrew across Cedar Creek and made a stand until attacked in the flank and rear. With Wickham's Brigade, Rosser flailed into the Federal flank, driving it back, sending its rear columns staggering, as Custer's main column forced its way across the creek pushing the Laurels before it. Now the Fourth Virginia attempted to sweep the Federal position, on a high bank, in their rear, but were met with a galling fire. The Fourth pushed on, hesitating several times amid the wall of fire coming from the high bank, but with a loud shout, charged and drove the enemy from its place as dark neared. Both sides, now completely exhausted, broke off the fight, Custer returning to Sheridan, with a victory, by Federal accounts. Rosser went into camp at Fisher's Hill. See McDonald, *A History of the Laurel Brigade*, 314–18.

11. New Creek is known today as Keyser, the county seat of Mineral County, West Virginia. It was located on the Baltimore and Ohio Railroad a distance of about twenty-two miles from Cumberland, Md. It was a village with only a few houses and the train station at the foot of the picturesque Alleghanies. However, it was considered an important junction by the Union army with two forts overlooking the depot. Both were situated on commanding hills, one, Fort Kelly, with over 1,000 men, huge food stores and ammunition and heavy ordnance. Two previous attempts at capture by Confederates, under McCausland and Fitz Lee, had failed. See McDonald, *A History of the Laurel Brigade*, 321–23. Major McDonald rode by Limestone Branch to Piedmont with his Eleventh Cavalry Regiment, approaching from the east. General Payne, with the Fifth, Sixth, and Eighth Regiments, took another road. On the way a casual conversation with a wayside resident revealed that a body of horsemen had left New Creek on a scouting mission and were expected back in a few hours. Payne decided to play a little trick on the Federal pickets and the neighborhood.

Dressing twenty men in blue overcoats and placing them in the advance of the column he rode boldly down the road at a walking pace and when in sight of the pickets approached them coolly. Along the New Creek Turnpike the Confederates moved on the road that was perfectly level and almost straight. The Union people living along the line of march came out to watch and assumed it was a Federal patrol passing as they observed the blue uniforms. However, when the main body rode into sight in its butternut uniforms it was too late for them to ride to the post and spread a warning. Those that attempted to do so were "taken care of." See McDonald, *A History of the Laurel Brigade*, 325–27.

12. Custer advanced with his division, 3,000 strong from Winchester toward Staunton as Sheridan was conducting a raid on the Virginia Central Railroad. Merritt's and Powell's divisions crossed the Blue Ridge at Chester's Gap and moved toward Charlottesville. Custer set out toward Staunton to occupy Early. Through his signal corps, Early learned of this movement and in the midst of a hailstorm he moved Wharton's Division toward Harrisonburg and Rosser, with all of the cavalry he could collect, to the front. Along with Payne, Rosser galloped through the mud and rain and about ten o'clock went into camp below Harrisonburg. Rations were not available for the tired horses who were called to service along with their masters in three hours' time as bugles sounded "to saddle," and the jaded column moved out to seek the enemy. Rosser knew that if Custer, who was in camp at Lacy's Springs, could remain untouched until dawn he would be too much for his small command; the only option presenting itself was an engagement before sunrise. Rosser, his men and horses moved quietly in on the Federals as cold winds blew, icy rain fell, clothing froze, and the mounts, not being rough shod, travelled with great difficulty. As Rosser writes, the first camp that was overrun was one of many that were scattered about the countryside and the small arms' fire alerted the others who mounted and formed column. Rosser felt elation as he and his men had forced into retreat a body of cavalry five times his numbers. Custer, with Staunton as his goal, did not get within forty miles of it. See McDonald, *A History of the Laurel Brigade*, 331–33.

13. Apparently Early didn't object too tenaciously to Rosser's mission. In his memoir notes that Rosser's mission was of great difficulty, but he captured the place along with 500 prisoners and some stores, and with only slight losses. Colonel Cook, of the 8th Virginia, lost his leg and had to be left behind. See Early, *Jubal Early's Memoirs*, 459.

14. Most of the Laurel Brigade was beginning to realize what the future held for them and the Southern Cause. Chilled and worn out by winter action, bloodletting, and worn by privations, they knew that even successful campaigns were leading nowhere. Previous raids, fights picked, and isolated raids that once were their delight and pride, were of no importance at this point in time. To win the struggle would require a great army with great leadership, leading to decisive wins. The Confederates found themselves greatly overmatched and outmanned by an enemy army that continued to add to its swelling ranks, with no end of manpower in sight. The last remaining light to which their eyes were fixed was General Robert E. Lee. Willing to give their lives to his keeping, each man stood ready to follow their great commander with unquestionable confidence. See Myers, *The Comanches*, 364–65. As to the amusing incident in which an enemy captain was hidden under the bed Rosser rested in, he said at the time of writing his accounts, that he had forgotten the name of the officer, but he had met him in Baltimore shortly after the war. The accuracy with which he related all the details left no doubt in Rosser's mind that he indeed was the man. Footnote in Rosser's writings.

CHAPTER 5

1. As soon as Sheridan started from Winchester, Early was warned by his signal and telegraph. He wired Lomax, headquartered in Millboro, forty miles west of Staunton, what to expect. Rosser was also told to gather all the men he could find. Early moved from his base at Staunton will all stores that could be moved. Early placed two brigades in position on a ridge west of Waynesboro to secure the removal of five pieces of artillery for which there were no horses and present a bold front to Sheridan. Early does not mention the conversation with Rosser, but in his memoirs he says he intended to hold the enemy until dark, then cross the river and take position in Rockfish Gap. The resulting attack on Early by Sheridan was a farce. The Federals got in behind him and also worked their way between him and the nearby mountains. His men surrendered by the hundreds. Early escaped capture by riding into another wooded area and later to the top of a hill and witnessed the greater part of his command being marched off as prisoners. See Early, *Jubal Early's Memoirs*, 461–63.

2. Pickett realized that he was greatly outnumbered by Sheridan and the U.S. Fifth Corps. As the battle at Five Forks loomed, the last act of the Confederacy was about to be played out, leading to the surrender of the Army of Northern Virginia in less than two weeks. See Long, *The Civil War Day by Day*, 660.

3. Grant believed Five Forks was of great importance in protecting his right and his assumption that the Confederates would fight vigorously for it was right. He also feared Lee's possible link-up with Johnston, in North Carolina. He sent Sheridan with two corps to turn the enemy's right: not to attack him in its entrenched position but to force him out if possible. It took two days. Lee directed his officers to "Hold Five Forks at all cost!" A loss there, he knew, would threaten his left and the army's entire line of retreat from the lines at Petersburg and Richmond. Thus, he thinned out his lines by sending over 10,000 of his jaded and hungry men to the forks where Pickett's men were dug in singing "Annie Laurie," and "Dixie." A large force of Federal infantry and most of its cavalry was dispatched. Brevet Brigadier General Horace Porter records that as he rode toward Five Forks to advise Sheridan of Grant's orders to send in Warren's Corps, he heard among the sounds of heavy firing one of Sheridan's bands playing. The sounds of "Nellie Bly" filled the air in a jaunty delivery, since the cavalry officer had always made good use of music which he believed lifted the spirits of his men. These musicians were mounted on gray horses and instead of being relegated to the rear ranks for the usual duty of carrying off the wounded and assisting the surgeons, they were brought out in front and made to play lively airs. But, after several of their instruments were pierced by shells and a drum crushed, its performance seemed a bit open to criticism. Warren was late and with Grant's permission, Sheridan removed him from command of the Fifth Corps. Later, he was cleared of all charges. Five Forks split Pickett off from the main Confederate army. Lee's right was crushed. Grant almost encircled Petersburg south of Appomattox Station, thus placing Grant close to the vital South Side Railroad, a vital line of supply for Lee. At this point Lee's army numbered a pitiful 10,000. At Five Forks it took 1,000 casualties and had 4,500 captured! This news of Lee's disaster soon spread like wildfire through the army. See Long, *The Civil War Day by Day*, 661–62; General Horace Porter, *Campaigning with Grant* (New York: The Century Company, 1897), 430–35; McDonald, *A History of the Laurel Brigade*, 367–68; Herman Hattaway and Archer Jones, *How The North Won. A Military History of the Civil War*, The Board of Trustees of the University of Illnois, 1983, 672. Longstreet defended Pickett, saying after the war that his position was not of his own choosing, rather from orders, with the understanding that he would be reenforced. Sadly, they arrived after his battle

had been lost and his command disorganized. He also points a finger at the cavalry on Pickett's left for failing to give advance warning of the enemy's approach. See James Longstreet, *From Manassas to Appomattox: Memoirs of the Civil War in America* (Secaucus, N.J.: Blue and Gray Press, 1985), 600–02.

4. Major General Bushrod Rust Johnson, along with Longstreet, besieged General Burnside at Knoxville. When the siege was lifted as Major General William T. Sherman approached, Longstreet returned to the East and Johnson joined Robert E. Lee's army to serve at Bermuda Hundred and the Crater, at Petersburg. Johnson served in Lt. Gen. Richard H. Anderson's Corps. His division included the Virginia brigade of Brig. Gen. Henry A. Wise; the South Carolinians of Brig. Gen. W. H. Wallace; Brig. Gen. Young M. Moody's Alabamians and the North Carolinians of Brig. Gen. Matthew W. Ransom. See Faust, *Historical Times Encyclopedia of the Civil War*, 397; *Battles and Leaders*, 4:752–53.

5. On this day, April 3, 1865, Union troops occupied Richmond and Petersburg. In the Confederate capital a Massachusetts soldier raised a small guidon over the State House. As many people filled the streets of the city, still in flames, they were jubilant. Negroes danced about and welcomed black Union troops who entered the city singing "Dixie" and "Kingdom Coming." Federal soldiers paraded through. A band played "The Girl I Left Behind Me." Looters were everywhere. At Petersburg in the home of Mr. Thomas Wallace, at 21 Market Street, General Grant and his staff dismounted and awaited the arrival of President Lincoln, accompanied by son "Tad" and Admiral Porter. The president expressing his jubilation to Grant for his successes. See Porter, *Campaigning with Grant*, 451–52; Long, *The Civil War Day by Day*, 665. When the Laurel Brigade learned of the capture of Petersburg, they, like many in Lee's dwindling army, began to lose faith in their commanding general. Petersburg, combined with the loss at Five Forks, deepened its sorrow. Grant, they believed, would prevail in the end, and only time would determine the end. After the fight at Deep Creek, Rosser went into camp at Tabernacle Church. See McDonald, *A History of the Laurel Brigade*, 367–68.

6. McDonald described the action at the springs as violent and that it did not provide an opportunity for the Confederates to reform their lines. McGuire's men rode among the enemy slashing wildly on all sides and chased them back to Jetersville. While the Federals lost heavily in manpower, the Confederate loss was smaller but most costly in the loss of McGuire and Rutherford, as Rosser noted. McGuire was a youthful 23 years of age. Also wounded were General Dearing, Major James W. Thompson of the horse artillery, and Captain Foxhall Dangerfield of the 7th Virginia Cavalry, all of whom had their wounds bandaged and fought again the next day. Fitz Lee reported 30 of the enemy were counted dead, mostly from sabre wounds and 150 wounded and captured. See McDonald, *A History of the Laurel Brigade*, 373–74. Word circulated among the Federal troops that Confederate President Jefferson Davis and his cabinet had passed through Burkeville, on their way south. Davis did meet with Johnston but found him, and Beauregard in no mood to conduct a guerrilla war. After the war, rumors blamed Davis' movement on the rail line for the delay in getting desperately needed supplies to Lee's army. Most likely it was the confusion and chaos of the last days of the Confederate government. Grant's raids on Southern railroads cut away at Confederate supply lines. Some factories were producing war needs and storehouses had them stacked, but they could not be moved. Meanwhile, the noose around Lee was tightening with the arrival of Sheridan and his men at Jetersville, blocking Lee's use of the Danville Railroad south, and a hoped-for connection with General J. E. Johnston, in North Carolina. If the two were to join, they could have attacked Sheridan. And, the two would have been reenforced and with Grant far from his supply lines and in hostile territory, he may have been

driven back. Grant camped on the night of the fourth at Wilson's Station on the South Side Railroad, twenty-seven miles west of Petersburg. At noon of the next day he was at Nottoway Court House. See Porter, *Campaigning with Grant*, 453; Long, *The Civil War Day by Day*, 666; Longstreet, *From Manassas to Appomattox: Memoirs of the Civil in America*, 610; Hattaway and Jones, *How The North Won. A Military History of the Civil War*, 670, 675–76.

7. On the night of the fifth Grant's hungry forces marched in all directions trying to get a handle on Lee's hungry, jaded and frustrated army. His objective was to prevent Lee's movement south and west. A part of that plan was to destroy the High Bridge over the Appomattox, with the assignment given to Washburn and his two regiments. Rosser and Munford fought with greatly reduced numbers. Dearing and McCausland assaulted the Federal right flank. Then the headlong rush and charge by Dearing at Washburn, who had been schoolmates at West Point, but did not recognize each other as they struggled. Washburn was felled by a bullet as was Dearing, who fell while discharging his pistol at Reid. When the bloody struggle ended, Rosser counted 780 Federal prisoners. Major James Thompson, of the artillery, whose guns were hampered by the impassable roads, had for two days fought with the cavalry. He fell while pursuing fugitives after the onset of the High Bridge at Farmville. Wounded in several places, his death came with a ball that penetrated through the vertebra of his neck. See McDonald, *A History of the Laurel Brigade*, 374–77. The last major engagement of the war occurred this day at Sayler's Creek, east of Farmville. Lee's army was now greatly fragmented. In the bottom land of the creek it split, with the forward sections moving on unaware that the back half, under Ewell and Anderson, had lost contact. Federal pressure forced the surrender of this half of Lee's army, numbering about 8,000. See Long, *The Civil War Day by Day*, 667–68.

8. The rear guard of Lee's army trudged into Farmville, in Prince Edward County, at about noon on the seventh. Rosser clung to the area like a bulldog. The enemy was resolved to give up on a frontal assault and resort to flanking movements, that failed despite their superiority in numbers. During these operations a Federal brigade approached White's people. Its commander determined wrongly that the Confederates, were a part of his own force and sent a courier forward with orders to not advance to far ahead of their supports. White, not at all interested in support, made no attempt to obey the courier's order and only pointed his pistol at his head with a demand for surrender that was obeyed. As the bridge over the river was destroyed and White's men took up the rear position they were hotly pursued with many having to swim the waters to get away. The enemy was so close that Company A was nearly captured to the man. See Myers, *The Comanches*, 382–83. On this date, the seventh, a number of the principal officers in the Army of Northern Virginia signed their names to a note urging General Lee that in their opinion there was no point in offering further resistance. General Pendleton made the delivery. After nightfall of the same day the first note from General Grant to General Lee arrived asking for his army's surrender. Lee replied asking what terms would be offered. See Longstreet, *From Manassas to Appomattox: Memoirs of the Civil War in America*, 618–19.

9. As the Confederates moved westward, away from Farmville, the men collected some oats stacks to feed their haggard horses at the first stop. Colonel White and Captain Myers each were observed holding a sheaf of oats before them. The men were scattered about the countryside, there being no thought that the enemy, believed to have stopped at Farmville, would be once again active in pursuit. Suddenly, Rosser and some of his men charged out of a nearby woods with some Federals chasing him. White instantly drops his oats and ordered a charge against the enemy, driving it back on the main body commanded by General Gregg. Rosser and his smaller force held the enemy in

check until Fitz Lee and his men rode onto the field. The two joined forces and drove the Yanks back again, and captured Gregg in doing so. It is interesting to note that Gregg made the same mistake as the courier to Colonel White. He tried to persuade a body of "Confederates" who were chasing his men to "halt and form." He realized his mistake only after it was too late. See Myers, *The Comanches*, 383–86.

10. At dawn of the ninth, the cavalry corps consisted of no more than 2,400. It went into position on the right of Gordon's infantry, a very short distance west of Appomattox Court House, with Rosser's division in the center. His men participated in this last cavalry charge of the war, driving the enemy off the field again. Reaching the Lynchburg Road he wheeled his men about, preparing to fight again, However, in the distance white flags were seen and soon thereafter men of both sides began to freely mingle. Without a moment of hesitation, Rosser turned his men toward Lynchburg where the Laurel Brigade was disbanded by Colonel White. See McDonald, *A History of the Laurel Brigade*, 381.

BIBLIOGRAPHY

Battles and Leaders of the Civil War. Vol. 4. Secaucus, N.J.: Book Sales, Inc., 1985.

Casler, John O. *Four Years in the Stonewall Brigade.* Edited by James I. Robertson, Jr. Dayton, Ohio: Press of Morningside Bookshop, 1982.

de Grummond, Lea and Lynn. *Jeb Stuart.* Pelican Publishing Co. 1979.

Dowdey, Clifford. *Lee's Last Campaign.* New York: Bonanza Books, 1960.

Early, Lt. Gen. Jubal Anderson. *Jubal Early's Memoirs.* Baltimore, Md.: The Nautical & Aviation Publishing Co. of America, 1989.

Faust, Patricia L. *Historical Times Encyclopedia of the Civil War.* New York: Harper and Rowe, 1986.

Freeman, Douglas Southall. *Lee's Lieutenants.* Three volumes. New York: Charles Scribner's Sons, 1942. (Freeman, *LL*)

Freeman, Douglas Southall. *R. E. Lee.* Four volumes. New York: Charles Scribner's Sons, 1935. (Freeman, *REL*)

Gallagher, Gary W. *Struggle for the Shenandoah.* Individual essays by Gary Gallagher, Jeffery D. Wert, A. Wilson Green, Robert K. Krick, and Dennis E. Frye. Kent, Ohio, and London, England: The Kent State University Press, 1991.

Garnett, Theodore S. *Riding with Stuart.* Shippensburg, Pa.: White Mane, 1994.

Hattaway, Herman, and Archer Jones. *How The North Won. A Military History of the Civil War.* The Board of Trustees of the University of Illinois, 1983.

Humphreys, A. A. *Gettysburg to the Rapidan. The Army of the Potomac, July 1863 to April 1864.* New York: Charles Scribner's Sons, 1883.

Long, E. B., and Barbara Long. *The Civil War Day by Day*. New York: Da Capo Press, 1971.

Longstreet, James. *From Manassas to Appomattox: Memoirs of the Civil War in America*. Secaucus, N.J.: Blue and Gray Press, 1985.

Matter, William D. *If It Takes All Summer*. Chapel Hill and London: The University of North Carolina Press, 1988.

McDonald, Capt. William N. *A History of the Laurel Brigade*. Gaithersburg, Md.: Old Soldier Books, Inc., 1987.

Myers, Frank M. *The Comanches*. Gaithersburg, Md.: Kelly, Piet and Co., 1871.

Porter, General Horace. *Campaigning With Grant*. New York: The Century Company, 1897.

War of the Rebellion: A Compilation of the Official Records of the Union and Confederate Armies. 4 series, 70 volumes, 128 parts. Washington D.C. 1880–1901. *(OR)*

112